Praise for *Multi-Family Millions*

If I didn't know better, I'd say Dave Lindahl has a degree in psychology.

This book shows you how to get inside the heads of real estate brokers, sellers, tenants, and buyers. When you follow Dave's advice in this book, your deals will become irresistibly attractive to the people you're negotiating with. Well done!

—Bill Bartmann, named "One of the Top 100 Entrepreneurs of the Last 100 Years" by the Kauffman Center for Entrepreneurial Leadership (www.BillBartmann.com)

Let's get real: There are hordes of real estate investors out there. These days the chances are slim of finding a deal with fat, obvious profits.

That's where this book is so crucial: Dave Lindahl shows you how to uncover the deals with fat, hidden profits that your competition will walk right by.

—Jeff Adams, President, www.RealEstateWebProfits.com

No theory here! Dave's book is filled with the practical steps you need to go from where you are to landing your first major deal. It just doesn't get more "connect the dots" than this.

—Stacy Kellams, President, www.RealEstateCourseReviews.com

So many books are just a bunch of vague generalities. Not the book you're holding in your hands: Dave Lindahl details the numbers investors need to get comfortable: specific ratios, rules of thumb, and tons of concrete examples. Add in Dave's easy-to-understand conversational style, and you have a winner.

—Wendy Patton, best-selling author of *Investing in Real Estate with Lease Options & Subject Tos* and *Making Hard Cash in a Soft Real Estate Market* (www.WendyPatton.com)

Dave Lindahl delivers the goods again. This step-by-step book shows you how to find almost secret deals with big hidden profits, and you won't even have any competition. It just doesn't get better than that!

—J. P. Vaughan, publisher, Creative Real Estate Online (www.creonline.com)

Multi-Family MILLIONS

Multi-Family MILLIONS

How Anyone Can Reposition Apartments for Big Profits

DAVID LINDAHL

John Wiley & Sons, Inc.

Published by John Wiley & Sons, Inc., Hoboken, New Jersey.
Published simultaneously in Canada.

For general information on our other products and services or for technical support, please contact our Customer Care Department within the United States at (800) 762-2974, outside the United States at (317) 572-3993, or fax (317) 572-4002.

Wiley also publishes its books in a variety of electronic formats. Some content that appears in print may not be available in electronic books. For more information about Wiley products, visit our web site at www.wiley.com.

Library of Congress Cataloging-in-Publication Data:
Lindahl, David.
Multi-family millions: how anyone can reposition apartments for big profits/ David Lindahl.
p. cm.
Includes index.
ISBN 978-0-470-26760-8 (cloth)
1. Rental housing—United States. 2. Apartment houses—United States. 3. Real estate investment—United States. 4. Rental housing. 5. Apartment houses. 6. Real estate investment. I. Title.

HD1394.5.U6L56 2008
333.33'8–dc22

2007052400

Printed in the United States of America.

V006992_050818

To the memory of my grandmother, Mabel Bowser, who, after the loss of her husband Fred Bowser just two years after opening the Old Town Fish Market in 1950, raised four teenage daughters and a late-in-life baby boy while keeping that business operating well into the 1980s.

The lessons that my mother, aunts, uncle, cousins, and I learned while doing our time at that fish market left a legacy of "family first" and hard work for generations of Bowsers to come.

CONTENTS

ACKNOWLEDGMENTS

I'd like to acknowledge Jon Rozek for his infinite wisdom and tireless work ethic in getting this book written. Readers have Jon to thank for its existence. When I was first offered the project by Richard Narramore, Senior Editor at John Wiley & Sons, I originally planned to turn it down due to time constraints. Jon showed me the importance of getting this information into the hands of the public.

To my mother and father, Carl and Barbara Lindahl, who give their endless support on an ongoing basis and whose company I enjoy thoroughly.

I'd like to thank Jeff Lindahl, Daniel Lindahl, Tammy Beckwith, and Robert Campbell for their tireless support and work ethic. Without their efforts behind the scenes, this project could not have been completed.

To Justin Meszaros, fellow principal of the Bostonian Investment Group, of which he is CEO, and LMW Management, for being the engine behind the phenomenal growth that we have experienced in the past few years.

I'd like to acknowledge Barry Weaver, President of LMW Management, for bringing his incredible industry knowledge and systemization to our growing real estate portfolio and using his expertise on a regular basis to keep our assets performing at their peak.

To Joan Lindahl, Chris Bowser, Jeannie Orlowski, Beth King, Jennifer Crawford, Debbie Marino, Patricia McKenna, Jill Emond,

Amanda Elwood, Kim Diamond-Santo, Jim DeRito, Elise Keane, Lisa McCarthy, Amy Londraville, and Doug Curley for being the pistons that keep the flow of business coursing through the Lindahl Companies on a regular basis.

To my nephews and nieces, Patrick Lindahl, Collette Lindahl, Nicholas Beckwith, Andrew Beckwith, Jacob Lindahl, Jonathan Lindahl, Kyle Lindahl, and Shannon Lindahl, for filling my life with endless pleasure. It will be exciting to share each and every one of your successes as you grow into this world.

Finally, I am deeply grateful to all of the RE Mentor seminar attendees, support staff, and joint venture partners. Without you, there would be no life-changing seminars.

CHAPTER 1

A DIFFERENT APPROACH THAT CREATES HUGE REAL ESTATE PROFITS

Congratulations. You're now reading a book that can change the way you think and invest in real estate. And it's a change for the better, because there are big profits awaiting the action-takers who follow the steps inside this book.

I must warn you: I'm a contrarian. If you're looking to get the same old advice from this book that will reinforce all the other things you've heard about real estate, I will disappoint you.

Are you also a contrarian? If you are, you'll understand what I mean when I say that it can sometimes be scary to *zig* when everyone else is *zagging*.

But the biggest profits are to be made when you buy low and sell high. And to *buy low*, that means you're buying when everyone is telling you how crazy you are. When you *sell high*, you're dumping properties just when everyone else thinks the party's just getting started.

If you stick with me, get used to two things:

1. You'll feel like a head case when everyone else is telling you how you're investing wrong; and
2. You'll make a whole lot more money than all the naysayers and backseat drivers put together!

That money will allow you to have what I call *The Attitude:* You can do *what* you want, *when* you want, *where* you want, for *as long as* you want, and *with whom* you want!

After all, isn't that a great way to live your life? That's the freedom that serious wealth brings.

HOW THIS BOOK IS DIFFERENT

Not only am I a contrarian, but I'm also different from the vast majority of real estate *gurus*. I believe you'll find those differences to be a breath of fresh air.

I'm Not a One-Trick Pony

Some authors have done two or even 20 deals and made a few bucks. Suddenly, they become *experts*. I've done more than 540 deals, and now control more than $142 million in real estate.

Other experts have worked in one real estate market only. Here's the problem with that: What worked for them in San Diego might not work 2,353 miles away in Sandusky, Ohio.

I've been buying real estate across the United States for 14 years now. I've enjoyed good times, like buying an apartment complex that resold for a $4 million profit after only two years of holding it. I've also suffered through bad times, like when a city task force tore down one of my buildings without giving me notice and not compensating me for it. Fortunately, I had just bought it and there was no one living there at the time.

There's a saying: *To the person who has only a hammer, the whole world looks like a nail.* If a real estate guru knows only how to do, say, single-family rehab deals, then you'll be getting lots of advice on how they're *the best* type of deal to do.

No, you need an entire tool belt of real estate power tools, so you can apply just the right one for the task at hand.

This book will give you another extremely powerful tool to add to your belt: How to make money repositioning multi-family properties. Is it the best approach in every market, at any given time? No. Then again, no one tool will ever do that.

But I'm handing you a tool that can make you a great deal of money in markets throughout the United States.

My Techniques Will Make You Money in Soft Markets

Just like seasons of the year and the economy in general, real estate has its own cycle. When you listen to an expert who's made money in only one part of that cycle, you're taking a big risk.

Have you ever read a real estate investing book, been proactive, and started using the material only to find out that you couldn't get any deals done? It probably wasn't a flawed technique. Most likely, you were trying an okay technique in the wrong phase of that market.

What if *your* market is in a different part of the real estate cycle? What if you have no idea where your market is in the cycle?

My system is based on:

- Buying and selling properties in any market
- Using the right strategy for the particular phase a market is in to maximize your profits

There are four different phases of a market cycle. Some strategies will work great in one phase, while others will not work at all—until perhaps the next phase, when they'll be just the right ones to use.

You can continually make great profits in your own backyard as long as you know what phase your market is in, and what strategies you should use right then. I explain in this book when just the right time is to apply the techniques you'll be discovering.

I Assume You're Holding Down a Day Job, with Very Little Spare Time to Get Your Real Estate Career Going

When I first started thinking about buying real estate, I had a start-up landscaping company that kept me going from morning to night. I also had family obligations and was part of several community groups.

Many other systems assume that you have all the time in the world to invest in real estate. They assume that you can complete long lists of tasks so you can become successful.

How unrealistic is that?

I'm betting you're in the position I was: You definitely want to get ahead and break out of the 9-to-5 grind, but your *time tank* is running on empty.

This is where my system shines. I will show you—in literally 30 minutes a day—how you can get started on your way to enjoying a lifetime of prosperity.

Sure, once you have your sights on a great deal, it will take more than 30 minutes a day. But then, you'll be working on a great deal! Even then, I'll show you how to get the very most done in the shortest possible time. I'm a time fanatic, and you're going to benefit from that.

This is not a *get-rich-quick* scheme. You'll see big benefits quickly, but still, it will take more than one deal to reach financial freedom. Here's the great part: I've discovered that if you will do for three to five years what most people *won't* do, then you can do for the *rest of your life* what most people *can't* do.

Think about that: Having financial freedom in three to five years. It doesn't matter how old you are, or what color your skin is, or what kind of education you have or don't have. And I'm *not* talking about quitting your job now. (If you follow the steps, you should be able to do that soon enough, but that will be your choice.)

You'll soon discover—as many of my students have around the country—that when you follow the rules and steps in the order I give them, this is a very easy game to play. When you see for yourself how easy it is to make big profits on a regular basis, you won't want to stop!

I Assume You Don't Have a Bankroll

Most real estate books assume you have access to cash. You probably don't—am I right? I know I certainly didn't.

When I started investing in real estate, I had less than $800 in my bank account. I was 29 years old. I once had a depressing thought: It took me 29 years to save up 800 bucks! In reality, I owed more than $800 on my credit cards, so I was actually in the red.

I lived in a one-bedroom apartment. Had been there for almost eight years! Oh, I tried to scrimp and save my money, and tried to cut my expenses. My mom always told me I needed to live off a budget and write down everything I did with my money. (Boy, did I hate that.) Still, no matter how hard I tried, something always came up that brought me back down to even.

I realized if I was ever going to be a real estate investor, it would happen from a standing start, with no dough behind me.

Many of the buying techniques you will discover in this book require *zero money down.* It's not because there's some extra merit in doing no-money-down deals; it's because I discovered a wealth formula a long time ago. It goes like this:

The more properties you can control with the least amount of money out of your pocket, the faster you will become wealthy.

When I started investing, I had to use no-money-down techniques just to get going because I *had* no money. Then, after a short period, I created a ton of cash flow coming into my one-bedroom apartment. Within 14 months, I had more than $10,000 a month in positive, spendable cash flow coming to me, month after month, like clockwork!

That monthly cash flow very quickly became down payments for more properties. I began to fund my own deals and didn't need to get into deals with no money down, because now I had money!

Then a funny thing happened: As I got better at playing this game, I had more deals flowing in, and they were good ones. I started getting into cash crunches again! This time, though, it was not because I was broke, but because I was so successful.

I didn't just pass on those good deals; I reverted back to buying them with little or no money down, just like when I started.

Eventually—no matter how rich you are—you will run out of money to do all the deals you want to do. You will need to use other people's money to fund at least some of those deals.

Not only that, I also learned that if you always use your own money to get into a deal, you live your life in a feast-or-famine cycle. You feast after you sell a property and get a chunk of cash, but more often than not, you are in famine mode while your money is tied up in properties that are getting ready for sale or refinance.

And there you are, worried again about how you're going to pay your bills. Real estate was supposed to eliminate that feeling. Using other people's money wisely means you can avoid this cash-flow crunch.

Another reason to use other people's money is to be able to act very quickly. Once you're into my system and on a roll, you'll see a great property that will evaporate if you don't act right away. Even if you're rich, if your money is tied up and unavailable, you'll watch that sweet deal and sweeter profit slide into your competitor's hands.

I know what you're thinking: "Dave, I couldn't sleep one night, and saw that late-night infomercial guy shouting *No Money Down!!!!!* Isn't that just a scam? Don't banks require that you put 20 to 30 percent down on properties?"

Your statement is partly true: Banks usually do require you to put 20 to 30 percent down on property. But I will show you where to get that money to put down!

In Chapter 8, I discuss the many options for finding all the money you need.

My System Is Proven to Work Not Only for Me, but for My Students

Not only will I show you how to use my techniques, I'll also give you real-life examples from lots of people who started with no money, no experience, and no time.

Esther Bass from San Francisco, for instance. This 58-year-old widow took charge of her future and bought her first three properties with no money down. Now Esther gets over $8,200 in monthly cash flow! I will show you exactly how she did it, too.

Jacqueline Hughes from Los Angeles is another example. Jacqueline lost her husband defending your and my freedom. She was left with three young daughters, an empty bank account, and an apartment she could barely afford.

Jacqueline took the concepts you're getting in this book, and with no money of her own, bought two properties. They now give her spendable cash flow each month of more than $7,000! Oh, and she has equity (that is, potential profit) of more than $2 million! She tells me she's about to buy a horse farm to raise her daughters on.

This book will also show you the land mines you must avoid while you're doing your deals. I spent many years studying at the School of Hard Knocks. I'll tell you about the mistakes I made. By learning from those mistakes, you avoid making them yourself. This alone will save you tens or hundreds of thousands of dollars.

You Can Be the Next Real Estate Millionaire

They say that *success breeds success*. Each year, I present my techniques to beginning, intermediate, and advanced real estate investors through my seminars.

If I'm so successful, why do I bother to do these events? Great question. I'll be honest with you: I have all the toys I need. They've been fun to dream about and now to own. But like all toys, they eventually lose their sizzle and go up on the shelf (or in the driveway).

Now, what do I care about even more than toys? It's the amazing feeling of gratitude from other people who act on my step-by-step techniques and become financially free. It's a big ego boost, let me tell you! Plus I'm paid a fair price for my knowledge, and that's nice, too.

You have the chance to become the very next freshly minted millionaire. You have everything you need in your hands right now. Later, you'll want to take the step-by-step actions I explain. But for right now, just sit back, refill that coffee, and let's dive in.

CHAPTER 2

WHY INVEST IN APARTMENTS?

There are a great many different ways to invest in real estate: Just within the area of single-family homes, you can buy and sell through wholesaling, retailing, lease options, and subject to. You can specialize in foreclosures, abandoned houses, fixer-uppers, and pretty houses.

Then there are techniques for investing in shopping centers, land, warehouses, industrial properties, and office buildings.

But there is one form of investment that:

- Is less risky than the others.
- Has greater economies of scale.
- Has the potential to make you more money faster.
- Is just beginning a growth phase that hasn't been seen since the 1960s.

I'm talking about apartment buildings. They can be big (400-plus units) or small (two to six units). Regardless of the size you buy, *start buying them!*

This is what apartment investing can do for you:

Patrick LaBlanc, a 34-year-old engineer, decided that working for a corporation wouldn't make him wealthy any time soon. He attended my seminar on investing in multi-family properties. More important was that he *took action.*

He began to buy in a market in the northern part of the country. (I'm sworn to secrecy on this one!) Within two years, he became the owner of 11 small multi-family properties that are throwing off a positive *spendable* cash flow of almost $9,000 per month! That's over $108,000 per year. Patrick is no longer working *for* the Man; he *is* the Man! And he's just getting started.

This is critical: *Patrick doesn't manage these properties.* You do *not* have to be the stereotypical landlord to enjoy the profits from an apartment building. A qualified property manager does all the hard work. They take care of the tenants, collect the rents, pay the bills, pay the mortgage, and put a chunk of cash flow into Patrick's bank account every month.

APARTMENTS SET YOU FREE

Forget about the time you may have wasted up until now. Trash the guilt and handwringing that befalls people who say to themselves (or are told): *We're not that young anymore,* and *we're so far behind on our retirement savings!*

If you invest in apartments in the manner I describe in this book, you can make up for a great deal of lost time. In fact, you could be retired in three to five years!

It doesn't matter if you're 18 or 80; in three to five years, you could hang it all up and *not have another financial worry for the rest of your life.*

I'm not talking about just retiring from your job. If that's all you're after, it can happen within the first year if you go after the right deals! No, I'm talking about retiring from your working life!

With apartment buildings *you* can decide how much you want to retire on. Do you want to retire on $50,000 per year? I hope not, because that's just above the poverty line! How about $100,000 or $200,000, or even $500,000? Those numbers seem so big—for now. I'm going to show you a path to turn them into reality.

How Many Units Are Enough?

Here's what you need to know: Each one of those big numbers represents a number of apartment units. Once you've accumulated that number of units, you're done. You are done for the rest of your life, because that cash flow will come into your house, month-in and month-out for the rest of your life, if you do only the most basic care and feeding of your money garden. (And remember, you're not the gardener on his knees; you hire the gardener!)

Let's say you want to live off $100,000 per year for the rest of your life. (That number will increase annually as your rents increase). If you've ever been a tenant, you know that around the time your lease is due, you practically assume the landlord will notch up the rents. Now you're on the other side of that transaction, as the property owner. Don't disappoint your tenants!

As a very rough average, an apartment unit will cash flow around $100 per month or $1,200 per year (these numbers will vary, based on the deal, location, property type, and so on). When I say *cash flow*, I mean *spendable dough in your pocket.* Therefore, if you want to live off $100,000 in cash flow every year, you need to accumulate $100,000/$1,200 per unit, or 84 apartment units. Let me put it another way: Owning 84 apartment units could make you set for life!

Take Janet and Bill Schroeder from Connecticut. They purchased a multi-family property in Oklahoma City with no money out of their own pocket. (They found a partner to put up the money; more on that later.) Janet and Bill get positive cash flow each month of $6,100. That's $73,200 per year. They got so excited about what they just did that they went right out and did it again!

I like being conservative. (I think it comes from my Swedish roots. My father, Carl Gustav Lindahl II, has always been that way. That's probably how he could pay for the upbringing of my brothers, sister, and me. Thanks, Dad!)

So let's be conservative with your situation: Let's assume you have no money. Let's further assume you follow my step-by-step process in Chapter 8 and get money partners to put up the cash for your deals. Depending on how the deal is structured, you should get between 25 and 50 percent of the monthly cash flow.

If you got 50 percent of the cash flow, you'll now need to accumulate 168 units to be free as a bird. That's double the number of units compared to our earlier example, but the good news is you *put no money down*. Not a bad trade-off.

This math doesn't even take into account appreciation potential. While you're enjoying all that cash flow on a monthly basis, your tenants are paying down your mortgage! That means even in a real estate market with no appreciation, your property is building equity. If you're investing in emerging markets, your property will be appreciating rapidly at the same time your mortgage balance is dropping. That's very good news.

Let me make sure you have the right picture in your head: By following my system for investing in apartments, every month you can enjoy a cash flow that supports your lifestyle. While you're out having fun, your properties are appreciating. At the same time, your tenants are going to work each day to pay you rent, which is paying down your mortgage.

For example, you might buy a building for $1 million and hold it for 10 years. You're retired and using the cash flow to live on. After 10 years, that property might be worth $1,500,000 and your mortgage principal may be down to $700,000. Notice that even though you reached your cash flow goal 10 years ago and you're living very comfortably, you're actually $800,000 richer now! You have the option to take out a loan against the property and pull some of that equity out.

They must have been talking about apartment owners when they said: *The rich just seem to get richer.*

Great News: There's Less Competition

Most small real estate investors chase single-family houses. Most very large (corporate) investors chase commercial properties like office buildings and big shopping centers. That leaves a comfortable and profitable gap for you and me to step up and make our fortunes in between!

There is simply less competition when you buy apartments. The reason is obvious: Most people are scared away by the fear of dealing with tenants. We've all lived in apartments with bad tenants, after all.

If, for some reason, a few investors are not scared off by the (mistaken) prospect of dealing with tenants, those investors most likely avoid apartments because they think it takes big money to get started. Also incorrect.

Investors making fortunes in apartments treat the business like a business. Each property is handled separately: It has its own ownership entity, checkbooks, property manager, and maintenance staff. Each month, separate financial reports are created and reviewed.

That's where investors should be spending their time—reviewing reports and doing more deals—not in rolling up their sleeves and dealing with tenants.

Some people hear what I've just said and think: *Oh, so Dave's one of those slumlords who doesn't stay in contact with his tenants!*

I'm *half guilty* of that claim. It's true that I personally do not stay in contact with tenants; but I insist that my property managers do! Later, I'll show you how to find good managers that not only take all that work off your back, but also are paid right from property revenues.

If you are too much of a *do-it-yourselfer*, and think you'll save a few bucks by managing the property yourself, I have news for you: You'll be a burned-out statistic within two and a half years, on average. You'll hate your tenants, they'll hate you, the property will be deteriorating, and so will your former profit.

Then a great thing will happen: You'll be selling your property to me (or one of my students) at a great price, just because you *want out.*

The whole trick is to *buy* from these landlords, and not *be* one of them.

LET'S EXPLODE THE *NO-MONEY-DOWN* MYTH

You've heard the hucksters promote courses on how to buy single-family real estate and commercial real estate with no money down. Their techniques unfortunately are little more than someone getting lucky.

The truth? Banks will indeed finance only about 80 percent of the money needed to buy a property. But as you'll see later, there are a great many ways to get other people to put up the remaining 20 percent, for a share of the cash flow and profits.

Here's a real-life example: Ellen and Leonard Spaulding bought their first deal, a 118-unit apartment complex in Decatur, Georgia. They purchased it for $4,860,000. But first, they put together a group of partners and raised $1,400,000 needed to close the deal. At the closing, they walked away with $140,000 to do repairs to the property, and another check for $170,000 just for putting the deal together!

They later sent their son, Daniel, who is in college, to my seminar to learn these same techniques. I'm guessing Daniel will never have to work minimum wage after graduating!

Let's take a closer look at the Spauldings' deal: On *the day of the closing*, they walked away with $310,000. Please let that sink in: Not only did they not *pay* to buy this property, but they *were paid to buy it.*

How many single-family properties do you think the Spauldings would have had to do to make $310,000, let alone at the purchase? A lot. Apartment deals are a profit *multiplier.*

So on Day One, Ellen and Leonard are ahead $310,000. Each month, they must share the cash flow with their investors, who get 50 percent of it. The total average net positive cash flow after all expense and mortgage payments is about $12,700 per month.

Ellen and Leonard get $6,350 per month or $76,200 per year. What a country!

They project that this property will be a five-year hold (why sell?). At current trends, they project the resale price to be $6,600,000. That works out to a gross profit of $1,900,000. The Spauldings' half will amount to $850,000. On top of around $381,000 in cash flow while they waited those five years. So the first deal they did should be worth more than $1,231,000 in gross profits. Ellen and Leonard have figured out they don't have to do a whole lot of these deals to retire!

I'll say it again: If you will do for three to five years what most people won't do, you'll be able to do for the rest of your life what most people can't do.

More Myths about Apartment Investing

Myth #1: Start with Single-Family Properties First

One of the myths that I hear over and over again is you should invest in single-family properties before you can start investing in multifamilies.

That's simply not true. The people who perpetuate those myths must be selling courses on single-family investing, or else they are badly informed. They think a bigger-size property means more risk. Here's why that is not necessarily true:

If you have a single-family property and lose your tenant, you've lost 100 percent of your income. The second piece of bad news is that it typically takes two to three months to get a new tenant into a property.

That's two or three months where you are paying the mortgage out of your own pocket. Add that to your own house mortgage or monthly rent . . . ouch, that's going to hurt.

What if you must evict your tenant out of your single-family house? Depending on which state you are in, that tenant could live in your property for another one to six months and maybe longer! Add that on to the two to three months that it takes to get the next tenant in, and you're going to be really hurting.

With an apartment building, you've at least got other tenants paying while your property manager is working to fill the vacancies. If you have one empty unit in a three-unit building, you may not have any cash flow for that month, but you're probably covering your expenses and mortgage.

If you have a ten-unit building and a couple of tenants decide to leave, not only will the other eight make the mortgage payment but you'll still have some cash flow that you can spend or reinvest in other properties.

Here's an odd rule of thumb for you: Your apartment buildings should never be more than 95 percent occupied. Why? Because if they're 100 percent occupied, you might very well be charging rents that are too low. But at 95 percent, you're getting the maximum level of rents on pretty much the maximum number of units. (Naturally, this logic applies only to properties with lots of units; a three-unit property would not fit into this rule of thumb.)

For every renewal and every new tenant, you should be asking higher rent. You keep up this policy until your occupancy gets below 95 percent. Now you've found out what the market is willing to pay for rent in your building. You should now level off, and hold it there until your occupancy climbs above 95 percent, at which time you start the process again.

Myth #2: You Need Experience with the Smaller Deal

The so-called *experts* tell you to get experience with small properties first. Only then should you *graduate* to larger ones.

The true risk is in listening to misinformed amateurs (typically a relative or one's barber), who seem to advise going into smaller deals with more of your own money as a down payment, until you're talked out of investing in real estate altogether.

Whenever you're starting something new, there is a lot of fear involved: Fear of the unknown, of failure, and even of success. There's fear of looking stupid, and of hearing "I told you so" from your spouse. You're in a very vulnerable state. It's often easier simply to take the advice of others if it keeps you from feeling any of the fears I just mentioned.

I vividly remember how fearful I was when I was planning to buy my first deal. That deal didn't come for nine months. I don't mean nine months from when I began; I mean:

- Nine months after I had enough information to buy the property confidently.
- Nine months after I was ready.
- Nine months of procrastinating and catastrophizing (that's a Dave Lindahl word for imagining I bought a deal and everything went wrong!).

I found many good deals during those first nine months, but I got really good at letting other people talk me out of every single one! I even found deals for other investors so *I* wouldn't have to buy them!

I finally bought that first deal. What changed? I had first seen that deal five months earlier, and thought at the time it was a good one. Five months later, I happened to drive by that property. It was still on the market and it hit me . . . this was *the one*. I chalk it up to divine intervention that kept this property on the market for five full months until I smartened up enough to buy it.

As I write this book, I own close to 5,000 units. Had I not bought that first little property, I might still be out mowing lawns in the summer and plowing snow in the winter.

Two things will get you over the fear of doing your first deal:

The first is education. You must get enough knowledge so when you do that first deal, you're taking a *calculated* risk. Not a wild risk, but a risk that sits on the foundation of solid investing principles. You know what the numbers mean and how to analyze them. You know what to expect before the closing, how to do your due diligence, how to get the property inspected, and how to find your property manager. You also know the best strategies to exit the deal. You always want to have an exit plan before you enter!

If that sounds like a lot that you need to know, it really isn't. These concepts are all easy to learn, and remember, this is an open-book test, unlike in school! You're free to ask your mentor (like me) if anything is unclear. It doesn't take long to internalize these principles. Once you've got them down, you're ready to spread your wings and fly.

The second thing that will get you over your fear? It's *taking action.* It's spreading those wings and stepping off the roost.

You can have all the skill and knowledge, but if you don't take action, it's worthless. In case you're wondering how you'll do in those first tentative tries to fly, I'll tell you: You will fall a few times. That's right: You'll screw up. But so what! After all, you're taking *calculated risks*, and not betting the farm. What will separate you from the scores of wannabes is that you got out there and took action. You started and then stumbled. But then you got up, dusted yourself off, and again moved down the road in the direction of your dreams.

Myth #3: Multi-Family Properties Are Too Complicated

This is just a variation on the theme that multi-family properties are too big and risky.

Perhaps those naysayers never bought an apartment building, so they don't understand the species. Perhaps they just blundered into a property without having a plan and therefore they overcomplicated what should have been a simple transaction.

In reality, apartments are no more complicated than other real estate investments, or most other skills, for that matter. Remember when you started to ride a bike?

I remember when I took those training wheels off and my father finally let go of the back of my bike. I streaked over to Mr. McKenna's newly seeded lawn. I tore right through the protective string he had up to keep everyone off his new grass. After skidding here and there on the soft topsoil, I dumped the bike over, and left a perfect imprint of my body in the dirt. Let there be no doubt that David Lindahl was there!

After a few more tries, I got the hang of it. The neighborhood was safe once again!

Just reconcile yourself that when you're starting out, you'll be bad at the beginning. Then you'll get better and—if you stick with it—will be on the road to mastery.

I'll let you in on a secret: That process can be significantly shortened by not being so much of a *do-it-yourselfer.* One of my favorite quotes is from German Chancellor Otto von Bismarck, who said: "Fools say experience is the best teacher. I prefer to learn from other people's experience."

There's no virtue in having to make all the mistakes yourself. In fact, it's foolish to do that if you know that someone else has blazed the trail and discovered the best way.

The way I look at it, if you're open to learning something new, why not make it a type of real estate investing that can make you so much wealthier, so much faster than your typical single-family home investments?

This Is Not a Myth, This Is Reality: They'll Laugh First, and You'll Laugh Last

When I started investing, I wanted to get as much education as I could. I became a member of my local real estate investment association. (If you haven't done this; do it now. Just go to Google and type in *real estate investment association Ohio*, or wherever you live. They'll pop right up.)

For me, that group was the Massachusetts Real Estate Association, run by Mike Hearny. Mike's been investing for many years and is one of those dedicated people who's more than willing to share his knowledge to help others.

A core group of us went to *every* meeting. We networked, talked about new techniques, bragged about deals we did, and hunted for lenders to do our new deals.

I remember when I told them I was buying my first multi-family property. After they finished laughing, most of them told me I was crazy. They hauled out the tenant-nightmare stories. *(. . . and can you believe it? He had kept her head in his deep freeze for 14 months! . . .)*

They almost succeeded in spooking me enough not to buy that multi.

But I had a simple test: If I could get into the deal with no money out of my pocket and get cash flow every month, I wanted in. That was my philosophy. I wanted enough cash flow each month so I could pay all my bills and not have to worry all the time.

It came down to a simple choice: Not being able to pay my bills every month was a bigger fear than owning a multi-family property. The multi won.

Hey, it was only a small three-family property. But I was in the game! Within three months, I had three more of them. Within six months I had nine multi-families. By the end of that first year, I owned 11 multi-family properties!

Each one of those properties was cash flowing close to $1,000 per month. That meant I had over $11,000 coming into my tiny one-bedroom apartment, month after month. Talk about a contrast from just one year earlier!

My friends had been so skeptical because the market had been so lousy. It was the back end of a wave of appreciation that lasted for five to seven years. The market was exhausted. Builders had overbuilt, the market was oversupplied, and demand was at its lowest point.

Now, one year after joining that real estate investment association, I was doing better than a lot of the other people in the group! You see, they were buying single-family properties and flipping them. While they were getting big checks, they had to wait to get those checks.

To get a check, they had to buy a property, fix it up, and find a seller for the property. Sometimes it can be quick, but six months are usually required to complete that cycle. (Trust me: I know. I later got my contractor's license and rehabbed hundreds of deals.)

While they were waiting for their dinky properties to close, I was raking in all those cash flow checks . . . 11 grand and growing each month!

I was rolling in cash, but I have a confession to make: I was also committing the cardinal sin of multi-family investing: I was managing my own properties! Keep in mind that people *to this day* think that's the way to invest in apartments. At the time, there was no person to tell me otherwise.

I was in the tenant business for just over three years! The toughest three years of my life. I did learn a lot of valuable lessons along the way, though. I managed those properties until I had created my own set of systems that I could hand off to someone I would hire.

Once I did that, my investment horizons just opened wide! I could now buy properties two hours away—and eventually 2,000 miles away. I shake my head when I look back and realize how restricted my business was when I was a typical landlord.

Later in this book, you'll discover how to find and manage a talented group of people who will become your team. That will allow you to do deals all over the country, too.

While most of the other investors were still flipping single-family houses in the third year of their investing, I now owned over 20 multi-families. My buddies were making good money: between $100,000 and $300,000 per year. Old Dave was laughing every month like clockwork. Why? My cash flow alone was comparable to that, and that didn't count the several million dollars in equity I had built up.

Get this: I still lived in that one-bedroom apartment! The difference was that I now *owned* the building.

If you start by investing in multi-family properties the right way, you can become wealthier, faster. Simple as that.

OPPORTUNITY IS EVERYWHERE

Until you know what to look for, you really don't see the opportunity. But as soon as you finish this book, you'll see investment potential just about everywhere.

Remember when you decided to buy a certain model and color of car? It seemed a bit unusual, and just right for you.

You searched around for the best possible deal and got it. How happy and proud you felt when you drove the car off the lot! The day seemed brighter, the air was fresher, your face cleared up, and immediately you knew your love life was going places!

On your way home you passed another car that was the same model and color! Before you knew it, it seemed like Detroit had stopped making any other car but yours!

What happened? You became familiar with an object and no longer did that object sit in the blurry background of your world. It stood out sharply. When you discover how to find multi-family deals, they will jump into your consciousness, and beckon you to buy!

A Brief Overview of the Different Kinds of Multi-Family Housing

In every community there are many types of multi-family housing. Properties for low-income families are usually government-subsidized housing. Then there's housing for working people who can't afford a house. There is also housing for the working people who simply choose to rent instead of buy. Finally, there is luxury rental housing.

For each of these classes, there is a letter grade: A, B, C, and D.

A properties are the luxury ones. They are usually less than 10 years old. White-collar workers live in them. These people are usually renters by choice: They don't want the hassle of home ownership. Maybe they've been transferred to the community recently, or are soon to be married. Some of them travel a lot and have yet to settle down.

Class A properties are the most expensive, and are usually bought up by institutions (corporate investors).

B properties were built within the last 20 to 30 years. Their tenant base is a mixture of white-collar and blue-collar workers. Some are renters by choice and others rent by necessity.

C properties were built within the last 30 to 40 years. This is where you'll find many tenants that are renters for life. On the other hand, some tenants (like me at one point) are just starting out in life. As they get better jobs, they work their way up the rental scale.

C properties are where you'll find many *Section 8* or government-subsidized housing tenants. Many investors are afraid of subsidized housing. They fear that the tenants are really rough. Well I'm here to tell you . . . they are! *But only if you don't screen them properly*. It just stands to reason: If you don't look at people's background when you rent to them, you're going to get tough tenants.

You are more likely to get good tenants if you:

- Screen for prior evictions
- Require that they have been working for two years before renting from you
- Require that they have lived in the same residence for at least two years before moving into your property

Yes, you will have to screen more applicants to get the good ones, but it's worth it. Treat these people like the gold they are and they will stay with you *forever*. (By the way, it's not discriminatory to impose these screening methods; it's only discriminatory if you don't screen everyone using the same measures. That's not only wrong, but it will land you in some very hot water.)

When I first started investing in my hometown of Brockton, Massachusetts, 60 percent of my tenants were government-subsidized. I had good tenants . . . because I screened every single one of them.

These D properties are the worst. They are in bad areas and have bad tenants. There are usually drug dealers in the units and as soon as you get rid of one, another shows up to reopen the store.

You see beat-up cars in the parking lot and bars on the windows. It's not a place where you (or your property manager) will want to go to collect rents, even in the daytime.

You can make a lot of money with D properties. I've done it. They are management-intensive and to be honest, involve many more headaches than rewards. You can make just as much money buying a B or C property as you can a D, with much less wear on your nerves.

Believe it or not, you will make most of your money in B and C properties. C properties will generate the most cash flow, and B properties will throw off less cash but will appreciate faster.

Every town has an area where each of these types of properties is located. Determine the property class you want to invest in and start driving around the neighborhoods. (Later in the book, I'll show you how to do this in cities thousands of miles away, without leaving the comfort of your home!)

You'll start seeing these properties jump off the curb and wave to you. You'll see small ones (three to six units), medium ones (6 to 60 units), and large ones, (60 to 1,000 units).

In another chapter, I explain how to locate the property owner.

Foreclosures Are a Coming Wave

Another place you'll find great deals is through foreclosures. Multi-family properties get foreclosed on just like homes.

Some fantastic deals are to be had, all across the country. The owners have a thousand stories to tell:

- Perhaps they were too aggressive when they bought and the numbers didn't really make sense.
- Some tried to manage tenants themselves.
- Others went into the death spiral of holding off on repairs, only to have the good tenants leave and rents drop, which resulted in delaying repairs even longer.

The bottom line is the property went upside down. Now there is an opportunity to buy it at a discount and make some real money, real quickly.

I bought a three-family at foreclosure for $41,000 and resold it for $160,000 nine months later. I put $22,000 worth of work into it, but didn't do the work myself. The profit was still a home run!

I once bought a two-family for $2,000! I put $60,000 into it and resold that one for $140,000.

I bought a six-family foreclosure for $125,000, put a little work into it and resold it for $295,000.

There is *big money* in multi-family foreclosures.

BURNED-OUT LANDLORDS ARE GREAT SOURCES FOR DEALS

Many of the best deals are from burned-out landlord-owners. They never learned that multi-family investing is a *business* and any seasoned business has *systems*. If you follow the systems, you're usually successful. If you don't, you're usually not.

I mentioned earlier that landlords burn out because they try to manage the properties themselves. They work themselves to the bone dealing with tenants, being hassled, collecting rents, paying bills, and worrying about their properties. Unless you're Superman, that burnout process takes about two and a half years. For Superman, it's about three and a half years.

Don't let this happen to you.

You should be managing your management companies, not your tenants.

I have a process for finding good property managers, and then ensuring that they do their job. They must follow certain specific processes to keep them accountable for maximizing your profit, and maintaining your property. I touch on these systems throughout the book.

Now do you see why apartments can be such superb investments?

IN THE NEXT CHAPTER

Before we wade in to too many details on how to make your real estate fortune, I want to make sure we cover first things first. In the next chapter, I discuss the steps you'll take to buy your first deal.

CHAPTER 3

An Overview of How to Get Your First Deal

I'm actually a very conservative guy when it comes to investing. I like to stack the odds in my favor as much as possible. Does that remove all risk from real estate investing? Of course not. Anyone who tells you there is a *risk-free way to invest* is either a liar or a fool.

On the other hand, many investors take more risk than necessary. That's also dumb. They do deals that just barely work—on paper! When you buy a *squeaker* of a deal that barely works theoretically, and then must contend with the realities of delays, national events, crazy weather, and so on—now your deal isn't a squeaker any more. It's a dog. Perhaps a better image is of an anchor, tied around your neck and ready to take you down with it.

This book is about repositioning properties for great wealth. But my conservative process for buying means that you'll also have two other investment options for that same deal: Buy and flip, or buy and hold.

Here's the bottom line: If you buy right, you'll have several alternatives for realizing your profits. At the end of this chapter, I'll talk more about them. First, let's dive into the process you'll follow to acquire a property.

THE 14 STEPS TO ACQUIRING A PROPERTY

These are the steps you must take if you want to invest with the least amount of time, money, and risk—and for the most profit:

1. Decide what **size** buildings you want to start investing in.
2. Decide **where** you want to invest.
3. Determine **what types** of multi-family properties you'll buy.
4. Put your **team** in place.
5. **Market** to get your deal.
6. **Analyze** the deals.
7. Create the **offer** or letter of intent.
8. **Negotiate** the deal.
9. Create and **sign** the purchase-and-sale agreement.
10. Do your **due diligence**.
11. **Renegotiate** the deal.
12. Start your **financing**.
13. Choose a **management company**.
14. **Close** the deal.

Let's go through each step.

1. DECIDE WHAT SIZE BUILDINGS YOU WANT TO START INVESTING IN

What size building are you comfortable investing in? Notice that I said *comfortable*. I've observed something from teaching thousands of students in the United States and around the world: People get excited about doing big deals, but they also fear big deals.

They leave my live events with all the tools they need; they've talked to students who've done deals and are coming back for a refresher course; they see it's doable and catch Big Deal Fever. Some of them douse that fever with a giant bucket of fear!

That's the wrong way to get over the fever *profitably*. The correct way is to start moving and take action by doing a small deal. You just need to get in the game.

It doesn't matter where you start. You could start as I did, and only do three-unit to six-unit deals for the first four years of your investing career. It took me that long because I didn't have a book like this to get me to my goals even faster.

Once you have a comfort level with how all the pieces of this puzzle go together, you might graduate to medium-size deals—20 to 75 units. As I've already said, some people actually go out and do multi-hundred-unit deals as their very first one!

It certainly is true that the faster you go big, the faster you'll become wealthy. That's because it takes just as much effort to do the big deals as it does to do the little ones.

But at this early stage, you don't have any proof that all this stuff will work for you. You're vulnerable because so many people can derail your plans with well-meaning (and not-so-well-meaning) advice. So whatever you do, keep your eye on that goal and do what it takes to get *some* deal—however small—under your belt and in your bank account.

After you've tasted success with that small building, your confidence will be overflowing. The naysayers will become background noise, and then silent. You'll naturally start focusing on larger properties. Before you know it, you've got a portfolio of apartment complexes that are spinning off cash flow like a cotton candy machine with no *off* switch.

2. Decide Where You Want to Invest

Do you want to invest in your own town? Looking at the demographics can help you decide which cities to focus on, or avoid.

When I started buying multi-family properties in Brockton, Massachusetts, everyone told me I was crazy. Brockton was a shoe-manufacturing city with tons of empty factories. I know it's fashionable to talk these days about *overseas outsourcing*, but it happened in Brockton long ago. Shoe manufacturing went overseas, big time.

When the factories shut down, the tenants of those multi-family properties moved out to find work elsewhere. Landlords couldn't rent their units and they started giving the properties back to the banks in record numbers.

As more buildings became empty, the riffraff moved right in: squatters, drug dealers, pimps, pushers, and thieves became much more prevalent.

Soon this once-proud, predominantly Swedish city became a haven for foul play. Poor leadership at City Hall caused years to go by with no relief. (I talk later about strong leadership, and how to make that a key tool in your analysis kit.) Brockton's reputation grew worse and its woes got deeper.

I grew up in a small town right next to Brockton. Whenever we would drive through Brockton, I can still hear my mother say: *Kids, lock your doors!*

So Crazy Dave was buying in a city this bad. However, I knew the *entire* city wasn't bad. In reality, I was buying in the good areas of a bad city. I was also buying for much less than replacement cost and my buildings were cash-flowing. I was in heaven.

I knew many other investors who would invest in only the nice towns surrounding Brockton. Some of them did well also. It's up to you to decide where you want to invest; it doesn't have to be a city down on its luck to be a profitable investment. It does have to be an area you're comfortable with.

Once you've decided, it's time to take the next step. Before we do, I want to talk briefly about investing beyond your backyard, in *emerging markets*.

Sometimes your local area just does not hold much current promise. Fortunately, by using management companies, you can *invest anywhere*.

When big corporate real estate investors buy properties, do you think they buy properties only in the city that their headquarters is in? No, they invest in cities that will give them the highest return. The great news is you don't have to be a big company to do precisely the same thing.

At any given time, 20 to 30 markets in the United States are emerging. That means they look like beat-up, low-potential markets now, but the stage is set for them to explode. Investing in these markets will explode your wealth, too.

Some people get intimidated by the distance. They tend to be the hands-on landlords who are months or days away from burnout. They feel the properties are too far away to control.

I actually think that distance is a good thing. The farther away the property is, the less likely you will go over there and work on it, interfere with the manager, or talk with the tenants. Control freaks can't handle this advice. That's too bad, because they are giving up the majority of their potential profit to feed their need to touch their portfolio.

Remember what I said earlier: You should run these properties like a business, and I *don't* mean the landlording business. You can apply these proven systems all around the country in areas that will give you the greatest return.

Therefore, if your local market just doesn't seem workable, there's no excuse to dump your dreams of financial freedom through real estate. Your first deal can be a *remote-control* investment.

I discuss more about emerging markets later. Also, you may want to get my other book, called *Emerging Real Estate Markets: How to Find and Profit from Up-and-Coming Areas*, also published by Wiley.

Okay, now that we know where we want to invest, it's time to take the next step. . . .

3. DETERMINE WHAT TYPES OF MULTI-FAMILY PROPERTIES YOU'LL BUY

Please don't think that when I say *determine*, I mean you're deciding on something permanently. Instead, I mean that you have to pick a provisional target. You can easily change it later to adjust for what information is coming in. But the only way to invest is to *have a plan*, and all good plans have goals.

What you're determining in Step 3 is the subcategory of apartment deal you'll first go after. It will make your marketing easier, because the more you're searching for something specific, the more it jumps out at you when you find it.

I have another name for *subcategory of apartment deal:* It's *Value Play*. They're so important to your future great wealth that I spend a whole chapter on them later. But for now, these are the types of properties you should choose from:

- Burned-out landlords
- Bad management
- Properties that need repair

- High vacancies
- Low rents

I know what you're thinking: *Dave, I can spot properties that need repair, but how can I tell if an apartment has those other problems?*

It's a good question, but you're getting ahead of me here. I show you later how to work it so *the landlords tell you* which type of property they have. Isn't that nifty?

For now, pick one of these categories, just based on your general understanding of the size of building and area you've chosen in steps one and two.

4. Put Your Team in Place

The next step is to put together a team of people that will successfully get you over the goal line to complete your deals. Successful businesspeople surround themselves with specialists who have more knowledge than they do—at least for that specialty.

Real estate is *a relationship business*. These are the key relationships you will be establishing:

- Real estate brokers (as many as you can get working for you)
- Property management company
- Bankers and other lenders
- Attorney
- Appraiser
- Property inspector
- Insurance agent

No, you don't need these people all in place from Day One. But I'm giving you the big picture. By the time you've done that first deal, you will have created relationships with all of these team members. Once you've done a few deals, there will be even more positions you want to fill on your team.

In Chapter 13, we go over how to build this team and the qualities that you will look for in each one of these individuals.

The first people you should put on your team are brokers. They are the people most likely to bring you deals. That means we're ready for the next step. . . .

5. MARKET TO GET YOUR DEAL

Nothing happens until you have a potential deal.

Let me be candid: There are a great many investors who are in reality spectators. They love the world of real estate investing, and can soak up knowledge on a par with the very best sponges.

But they remain spectators because they never do the marketing to bring in a potential deal. This is the most critical—and most-often missing—step in your real estate investing path.

I own real estate across the United States valued in the *nine figures*. But I don't consider myself in the real estate business! I'm in the *marketing business.*

You will find good deals through effective marketing. You'll find lenders willing to do no-money-down deals through marketing. And you will employ other marketing techniques to sell your deals at a handsome profit to other people.

It doesn't matter how much skill you have; it doesn't matter how much knowledge you've accumulated: If your phone is not ringing and the mailbox is empty, you're not going anywhere.

I can't show you one way to get 20 deals, but I can show you 20 ways to get one deal! That should warm your heart because it means that you'll have a whole bunch of marketing tools to apply to any market at any time. Some will work better than others in San Francisco today, and the situation will be reversed in Atlanta. Next month, it may be still other techniques that are becoming most effective.

I'm going to create a pipeline of deals presenting themselves to you through the phone, e-mail, and post office. Once you've turned on that pipeline, never turn it off! It's your goose that's laying your golden deals. Deal flow is the engine that drives your business.

I cover marketing extensively in Chapter 5.

6. ANALYZE THE DEALS

Once you start getting leads coming in to your business from all of your marketing, it's time to separate the good deals from the bad. The majority of what you'll see in the beginning will be worthless deals. No big deal. It's just the nature of the beast.

Real estate brokers will test you. They'll first see if you buy the deals that they have in house that other investors have passed on. They'll throw lots of potential deals at you to see what will stick.

You must analyze each deal to separate the winners from the losers, and you must handle the brokers in a very specific way. They're worth cultivating, and later, I show you how.

Deal-making is like cooking: There is a tested recipe for buying an apartment complex. Follow that recipe and you've got something of value. If you've never followed the recipe before, and you think you know better, you may be tempted to tinker with it.

Do what you want with brownies in your kitchen, but when it comes to the recipe for making dough in real estate, just follow my instructions to the letter. When I'm on your yacht and you're telling me about your latest real estate conquest, I'll be impressed with the unusual techniques you employed. First get the yacht. Stick with me and I'll show you how.

In Chapter 7 I give you the tested recipe for deal creation. If you follow simple rules of thumb and run certain calculations, you'll put quality deals into your portfolio.

7. Create the Offer or Letter of Intent

Once you've got a deal that you think is a winner, it's time to make an offer on the property. After you finish this book, if you are not making regular offers on properties—I'm talking one or two a week—you are really not in the game.

As you'll discover later, the offer does *not* mean you will definitely be buying the property. It means that you're serious, and now want to see the real details behind the apartment complex.

When you are buying properties between 2 and 10 units, you will use a standard form to make your initial offer on the property. When you're buying larger complexes, you will use a Letter of Intent.

Both accomplish the same thing: They throw the ball over to the seller's court to either accept the offer or counter it. In most cases, the seller will counter the offer, which brings us to the next step. . . .

8. NEGOTIATE THE DEAL

When creating the offer, there are certain important strategies I'll show you how to employ. When you enter the negotiating process, you should position yourself so you can get to the best end result. That means following clear principles and steps I lay out for you.

You will determine at what maximum price you can buy the property. This is called the *strike price.* If you cannot get the seller down to this price, you then end the negotiations and move on to the next deal. (Remember, with your marketing keeping your pipeline full, there is *always* another good deal around the corner.)

The general rule of thumb is to start negotiating at 10 percent below your strike price.

Let's say a property is on the market for $550,000. You do your analysis and determine that you won't pay more than $500,000 for the property. That's your strike price. If you follow the rule of thumb, you will start your negotiating at $450,000.

Negotiation is a skill you can definitely pick up. In Chapter 8, I give you a straightforward process you can follow to emerge a winner.

9. CREATE AND SIGN THE PURCHASE-AND-SALE AGREEMENT

After the negotiation over price is complete, it's time to create the purchase-and-sale agreement (also known as the *P & S*). This document outlines exactly how you will buy the property and what the key dates will be.

The date on which both parties sign the P & S is called the *effective date.* All subsequent dates in the transaction are based on the effective date.

Not all purchase-and-sale agreements are created equal. If you allow the seller to provide the P & S, it will save you money with your attorney, because you will not be charged with the creation of the initial draft.

You'll also be making a profound mistake!

You should either use your attorney's P & S, or one that your attorney reviews and negotiates to protect your interests.

It's your attorney's job to get that document to favor you as much as possible. Of course, that's also the job of the attorney for the seller.

Your attorney will analyze the document and come up with a list of *exceptions:* items and wording that are not in your best interest to have in the document. You'll get a list of these exceptions and the negotiations will begin.

One common exception relates to key dates. Most deals allow 30 days for due diligence to be done and another 30 days to close the deal. This means you are closing the deal in 60 days. Be sure to surround yourself with a team that can meet this very short deadline, or you'll lose deals to your competition. The person who offers the same amount of money—but gets that money into the seller's pocket first—wins.

Whenever you can, try to get 45 days for due diligence and another 45 days to close. Doing everything you need to do to close on an apartment complex—and doing it right—takes time. Still, stay alert to whether your competition is offering to close more quickly; you may have to cave on this point to save the deal.

Another common negotiating point relates to the down payment. The seller will typically request between 1 percent and 5 percent for a down payment. The most common request for a smaller property is 3 percent to 5 percent, and for a larger complex, it's 1 percent.

This money is usually refundable until your due diligence period is over. At that point, it becomes *hard,* which means you can't get it back. You must *know your dates:* Miss a date and possibly lose some money.

Whenever possible, get a third party to hold the due diligence money (also known as the *down payment* or *deposit*). Your attorney is the best choice, but that rarely happens. The broker's attorney or title company is usually the third party; sometimes the seller's attorney will be required to hold the money. The one person who should *never, ever,* be allowed to hold the down payment money is the seller!

If you let the seller hold the money, don't expect to get it back, even if the deal doesn't close. Oh, you might get it back *eventually,* through a long court battle. Who wants to do that?

There's another reason not to allow the seller to hold the down payment: It puts you in a weaker negotiating position.

Let's say you've done your due diligence and found issues you were not aware of. You want to negotiate those issues with the seller. How motivated do you think the seller will be to negotiate if he's already holding your money?

Yet another negotiating point is the title work and the survey. In most cases, the seller usually pays for the *title abstract* work and for an updated survey of the property. More and more sellers are negotiating to have the buyer pay for these services.

You will usually be required to send over the down payment money within 48 hours of signing your P & S (or letter of intent).

The P & S is the most important contract that you'll sign before the closing. It's well worth the money to have your attorney actively involved on your behalf.

10. DO YOUR DUE DILIGENCE

Now that the ink is dry on the P & S, it's time to start doing your *due diligence*, which is a Wall Street term for your in-depth property research.

During your due diligence, you make sure that the deal you thought you were making an offer on is in fact the deal that exists.

Due diligence is broken down into three categories: financial, physical, and legal.

The first information you usually get when doing your due diligence is financial. As should be stated in your P & S, the seller is required to forward to you all the financial information you need within 14 days.

Here's a tip: When this information comes in quickly, the deal usually goes smoothly. When it comes in late, or in bits and pieces, either the seller doesn't keep very good records, or the seller is trying to hide something.

The information you're requesting is:

- Last three years of operating statements presented on a 12-month trend report
- Year-to-date profit-and-loss statement
- Balance sheet
- Last 12 months rent roll

We're highly focused on the income aspects of the property, because you created your offer based on the income. (I show you how to do that in Chapter 7.) It's now time for the seller to prove that income.

If the seller can prove the income, great: The deal continues forward. If the seller can't prove the income, it's time to go back to the negotiating table. You want a lower price that makes sense with the new information you now have. Some sellers will agree to renegotiate, and others won't. You must be prepared to walk away. Here's my broken-record speech again: That is why your marketing and deal flow are so vital.

After you've confirmed the financial information, you can start on the rest of your due diligence. Do not start any other part of the due diligence process *until* the financials are done, because the physical and legal due diligence will begin to cost you money.

If you walk away from the deal during the financial due diligence, the only money you have spent is your deposit, and you will get that back (assuming a third party is holding it, not the seller!). Any time during the due diligence period, if you decide for any reason that you want to be out of the deal, you get your deposit back.

The first thing you do when you start your physical and legal due diligence is to hire a competent attorney to do the title work. The attorney will check that what you *think* you're buying is in fact what you're buying. He or she will review the legal description, previous owners, how the property was transferred previously, easements, and mineral rights. You'll then receive a report. Either the deal is clean or it may have some issues that need to be resolved prior to closing.

A good attorney will make sure that all issues are resolved before the closing. That way, when you resell the property, you won't have any issues and you can collect your profit.

You then hire a competent engineer to do the physical due diligence, which is a property inspection. The engineer will check all major mechanical and structural systems. On larger properties, he will do a survey of the apartment units. On smaller properties, he will go into every unit.

When I say *survey*, I mean going into one out of every three units, or 1 out of every 10 units, depending on the size of the complex and what the engineer is finding.

If the engineer starts to see things he doesn't like, he'll go into more units. After you get the report, you'll set up a time for you to walk through every single unit on the property—if you're smart.

I know this can take a while. I recently walked a 344-unit property with another member of my team. It took two days, and my time is valuable. But we were spending over $9 million for the property and I was using other investors' money to buy the deal. I wanted to make sure I knew that property inside and out.

When you walk the units, what you're looking for is the *common problem*. Every property has a common problem. It's your job to find out what it is.

Perhaps it's the fact that all the faucets and handles are 20 years old and there are now repeated service calls to replace them, one by one. Maybe it's outdated or worn carpet; it could be older appliances that will need to be replaced on a regular basis. It could be fraying cabinet doors, leaking air conditioning units, or overflowing condensers. Every property has a common problem. Don't stop until you find what it is, and allocate resources to counter that problem.

While you're doing your walk-throughs, you should be talking up the staff. You should find out who's good or bad, naughty or nice among those property personnel. They don't realize it but they're actually in a job interview. You may be buying that property. There is no better employee than one who knows the property well and does a good job. There's no worse employee than one who knows the property well, and also knows how to slack off and steal from you.

During this walk-through process, you should mentally put current employees into these two categories, subject to later confirmation, of course.

The engineer or inspector will have to provide you with key information, such as what immediate repairs need to be done to the property, his estimate of costs, and, among other things, whether the property is properly zoned.

If everything works out okay during the inspection phase, then you're ready to get the financing. The inspection may have revealed problems that the seller didn't tell you about. I don't mean trivial stuff, which you can expect to find in every property. I'm talking about problems that will cost you a chunk of money: a bad boiler, a roof replacement, dry rot in the walls. If that's the case, it's time to. . . .

11. RENEGOTIATE THE DEAL

Another term for this is *retrading*. If you plan on buying a lot of properties and doing a lot of business with key brokers, you don't want to get the reputation of a *retrader*.

These are investors who will nitpick a deal and try to squeeze every last dollar. Sellers hate them and so do brokers. It's a pain in the butt for brokers to be going back and forth between the buyer and seller, endlessly settling small-potato issues.

Remember, they've got plenty of other investors out there to refer the next great deal to. Don't be a pain in the butt. Make doing business with you easy and you'll do way more business.

Of course, if something comes up that will cost you a chunk of cash, it's time to go back to the seller and say: "Mr. Seller, you didn't tell me that the boiler would need to be replaced. That's a $15,000 job. I'd like you to give that money back out of the sales proceeds at closing. That sounds fair, doesn't it?"

He will do one of two things: He'll give you the money at closing; or he will tell you where you can go. If it's the latter, then you have a decision to make. Is the problem a deal-killer? If not, then you'll need to eat that cost. If so, walk away from the deal.

Sometimes, you'll find that your walking away will make the seller want you back. Other times, you'll simply walk away.

Important tip: Did you notice that I asked the seller to give the money back at the closing? That's called a *repair allowance*. Beginning investors will ask the seller to reduce the price. This is a mistake. If the seller reduces the price, you'll still have to solve that problem! Now you'll be coming out of pocket to solve it.

If you have the seller give it to you at closing, then your financing will be funding that repair. Banks usually allow you up to 3 percent of the purchase price for such repair allowances.

12. START YOUR FINANCING

You will finance your deals from three primary sources: local banks, national lenders, and conduits.

Local banks are usually good for construction loans for multi-families. Their rates on regular loans are higher than other lenders, and their amortization schedule is usually shorter. (In other words, they want the money back sooner.) They typically write their loan over a 20-year period instead of a 25- or 30-year period.

If you are doing a construction loan for a repositioning, you'll need to use local lenders. Not only do they usually have good rates on such projects, but banks won't lend out of their geographical area for a repositioning; your only choice is the local guy.

You'll need a *construction loan* when repairs exceed 3 percent of the purchase price and you're planning on financing the repairs into the deal. You'll need a *bridge loan* when the property is less than 85 percent occupied. This occupancy level is called *stabilization.*

You get your best loans at the lowest rates when you are buying stabilized properties. These properties also typically generate cash flow from Day One.

I call cash-flow-generating deals *momentum plays* because you have momentum in your favor. Your property is stabilized and cash flowing the day you buy it. National lenders and conduit lenders love these deals.

National lenders are big enough that they don't hold on to all the loans they make. Instead, they sell some of the deals to *secondary markets.* The key secondary market players are *Fannie Mae* (Federal National Mortgage Association) and *Freddie Mac* (Federal Home Loan Mortgage Corporation). They buy mortgages from the national lenders, so those lenders can now fund even more deals. Fannie Mae and Freddie Mac are great to do business with. They usually offer lower rates to close the deals, but they like their deals to be *clean.*

They're looking for stabilized properties. They don't want to do a lot of repairs. One more thing: They like to see *pitched roofs*. They have a thing about flat roofs, because the flat design tends to result in more maintenance problems. They will finance properties that have them, but they won't like it. And remember: We want to keep our lenders happy so they keep on lending to us!

They also like to see an upward or stable trend in income for the last six months. This is called the *six-month trailing report.*

You may want to finance through a conduit lender if:

- Your deal is a little messy.
- The numbers aren't totally complete.
- You've only started to stabilize over the last two to three months.
- The property has a flat roof.

A conduit lender gets its money from Wall Street, insurance companies, and investment houses. Conduit rates will be a little higher, but they'll do deals that have a little *edge* to them.

You'd be wise to get a good mortgage broker on your team. Mortgage brokers will have a stable of Fannie Mae, Freddie Mac, conduit, and local lenders that they do business with regularly.

They will take a look at your deal and tell you right away who will finance it. They'll also fight for you get it done. For this, they are typically rewarded one point, or 1 percent of the financed amount. The good ones earn this point and you're paying for their experience.

If you want a good one, go to my web site at www.MultiFamilyMillions.com and put in the keyword *broker*. We'll refer one to you.

13. CHOOSE A MANAGEMENT COMPANY

While all this is going on, you should also be lining up your management company. There are many types of companies in any given market.

Surprise: Some are good, others are lousy. Just as with properties, you need a method to determine who's who. You'll be asking them pertinent questions about their experience, how they operate their business, how they plan to keep your property full, and how they will maximize your profits.

Some managers are really good at slinging the BS. My best advice is to start at the irem.org web site. IREM stands for the *Institute of Real Estate Management*. Go to this site and look for Certified Property Managers (CPMs) or Accredited Residential Managers (ARMs) in your area.

They are in every state and many cities. These people have taken many classes to earn the designation. A high percentage of these managers are very good. You're starting off with way better odds than if you simply opened up a phone book.

If managers don't have one of these designations, it doesn't mean they're not good; but you'll need to screen them very carefully.

Here's a valuable lesson I learned early on: Property managers specialize in certain properties. Make sure you match the property manager with your property type. Otherwise, you may have a highly qualified manager who still fails. How do I know this?

I bought a 41-unit property in Montgomery, Alabama. The neighborhood and tenant profile was C–. There were many Section 8 tenants, and the property had a lot of deferred maintenance. I was okay with this going in.

I had gotten referrals from several people in the area and they all said to use this one particular management company, because *"They are the best."* Usually when one name comes up over and over, it's a good indication that you've found a winner.

I hired the company. Three months later, my property was much worse off than when I bought it.

There were more vacant units, and my expenses were out of control! We talked about it many times. They were *certain* the property was just about to turn the corner and start performing. "Give it one more month, Mr. Lindahl," I'd be told.

Then I realized my mistake. This company was indeed expert at managing high-end properties. But mine was a low-end property. They didn't know how to attract that type of tenant base, and were over-screening the tenants. They also were repairing my vacant units as if the CEO of a company was going to move in.

When I asked them about this, they told me: "We have high standards, and we aren't going to compromise them." I told them that I, too, had certain standards, the first being that I make a profit while providing a safe, affordable, and clean place to live. If I don't make the profit, I can't provide the housing.

I had to replace that company with one that understood how to manage my type of property. The failing company gave me a very hard time and made it a difficult transition. If you're ever buying in the Montgomery market, call my office and I'll tell you who they are.

14. CLOSE THE DEAL

All the pieces are now in place. The only thing left to do is to finish the financing paperwork. You are ready to close the deal.

When you buy smaller properties, you'll close in the title office or an attorney's office. With bigger complexes in emerging markets across the United States, the lender will mail you a document package overnight. You'll sign it in front of a notary, and send it back overnight.

The seller will do the same. Then you wire the funds over on the appropriate day and you're the proud owner of the property. You now turn it over to the management company.

After you celebrate, you'll be dying to go out and do it all over again!

Now that you know the initial process, let's talk about the three options you'll have for converting that property into profits.

OPTION 1: BUY AND FLIP

When you're starting out, you have very little time and less money. One option, therefore, is to flip your deal for a quick profit.

When I say *flip*, I mean you put a property under contract, close on it, and immediately sell it to another party to realize your profits.

To flip a property, you must be buying the property *under* market value and you then resell it *at* market value to another investor.

Why would people sell a property to you below the market value? There are many reasons:

- They may have inherited a property they don't want or don't know how to run.
- They're in foreclosure.
- They could be in bankruptcy.
- They're a burned-out landlord.
- They see profits starting to drop and want to get out while they still can.
- It may be an estate sale.
- They could be trading up to a bigger property.
- They're retiring from the game.
- They need money quickly to fund another venture.
- They need money even more quickly to pay taxes to the IRS.

People sell below market value for these reasons and more. As you understand by now, I want systems in place to attract these motivated sellers continuously. I discuss those systems in Chapter 5.

Let's say you find a motivated seller of a three-family property. It's worth $375,000 but the seller needs to get out quickly and just wants what's owed on the mortgage. (It happens.) The mortgage amount is $311,000. You agree to purchase the property for $311,000.

You could make your profit on this property in two ways:

1. You could assign the property to another investor and get an assignment fee, or
2. You could close on the property and immediately put it back on the market to resell it.

The Assignment Process

Let's look at how the assignment approach works:

When you create the offer to buy the property, you put your entity name in as the buyer of the property. (*Never* buy in your own name, for asset-protection purposes.) After your entity name, you put the phrase: *and/or assigns.*

For example, when I'm buying a property, I usually buy in a limited liability company (LLC). For simplicity, I usually call the LLC by the same name as the street address of the property.

When I was a beginner, I went to a seminar on asset protection. The self-proclaimed guru told us all to be creative when naming our entities for properties we would buy.

He said to be creative so no one could figure out who owned the property. He also told us to name the entities so they sound like they are part of a bank, like First National Trust. That way, people who were trying to get to the owner of that property might think it's a bank. His said a personal-injury lawyer would be less likely to come after us if anything happened to a tenant on our property.

Being a good student, that's exactly what I did for my first nine properties.

What a bunch of malarkey that turned out to be! I had nine different properties with nine different names. I was so clever with the names that I got confused as to which property was which. I paid bills out of the wrong accounts and was constantly double-checking myself to make sure I was insuring the right property, or paying the water bill for the right one.

I finally got smart. Now if I buy a property on Market Street, I name the property *Market LLC.*

You may even buy two properties on the same street. In that case, just call it *65 Market LLC.*

When I'm buying larger complexes, I name the entity after the name of the apartment complex. If I'm purchasing the 284-unit Magnolia Park apartment complex, I name it *Magnolia Park LLC.*

That stopped the confusion and I stopped going to that guy's seminars!

Just be sure that whatever name you give to the LLC, add to the end: *and/or assigns.*

This allows you to assign the contract to a third party. You will receive an assignment fee before any closing, and the third party will close on the property.

The benefit to you? It's the very fastest way to get money after putting a deal together. The downside is you don't get the big lump sum that might be yours from the property down the road.

The size of your assignment fee depends on how well you negotiated the deal, and how much equity is in it.

On smaller properties, most investors will not buy from you unless they're making at least $20,000 on the transaction. That's the low end.

Thus, if you want to make a $5,000 assignment fee, you'll need at least $25,000 in equity. When I say *equity*, I mean the net amount of proceeds in the deal after taking the market value and deducting any costs associated with it.

Most assignment fees are between $5,000 and $10,000 on smaller deals and as much as $100,000 to $500,000 on bigger ones. Not bad, huh.

I'm currently working on a deal where I'm being asked to pay a $1.2 million assignment fee to someone. It's a very big deal: A $52 million portfolio. The person holding the contract is willing to wait for his $1.2 million until *after* we close. That's good, because I can now finance that right into the deal, as you already know from our previous discussion.

Over a million bucks is a big fee, no doubt about it. But I have the potential to make 10 times that amount. Would I therefore give up $1.2 million to make $10 million? All day long!

That example brings up an interesting point: When *you* are assigning a contract over to a third party, *never* wait until the closing to get your assignment fee! I know, I just told you that my guy is waiting for his $1.2 million. But here's an extremely important principle for you: *We do not sell the same way we buy.*

You should not wait because you want your buyer to have some *skin in the game.* You want him to put up cash so there is a high probability he will close.

If not, there's nothing stopping him from walking away from the deal, even on the day of closing. I've seen it happen. Then you'll be stuck with the contract and any penalties that might be imposed.

Here's the other reason you want the seller to pay the assignment fee beforehand: If he doesn't, he may decide to renegotiate with you as you are getting close to the closing. If this happens, you'll be negotiating from weakness: You need him to close to get that deal done and get your money.

Before you know it, he'll negotiate you down, and your finder's fee will evaporate before your eyes. You'll be smarter for the lesson you just learned; then again, why don't you just learn the lesson from me right now?

The only time you should assign a deal is if you need money quickly, or you're so busy doing other deals that you don't have time to do anything more with this one.

That's okay, because you never, ever want to shut down that deal pipeline, remember?

The Quick-Sale Process

If you do have more time, then by all means try to stick with the deal and get that pot of gold that's waiting at the end of the rainbow.

The way to do that is to take the deal through closing, and then sell at the market rate. So instead of having to assign the deal to someone who will make his profit by selling it at market rate, you'll get that profit, too. It will mean that you have to arrange your financing, and close, and then prep the property for resale (most likely cosmetic repairs).

This is still a flip, because you're not holding on to the property for any length of time. It's just that for your work in closing the deal, you get more profit.

If you're smart, you will begin the marketing process to sell that property *as soon as you get it under contract.* Not after you own it, but just after you have it under contract. If you're lucky, you may be buying the property from the seller and selling it to your buyer on the same day! That's called a *double closing* or *simultaneous closing*.

The double closing is great, but don't count on it. Buy your property with good enough numbers in place that it's generating cash flow. That way, you won't be coming out of pocket to hold the property before you sell.

Single-family homes are nice investments, but this is so much nicer! With an empty single-family house, you pay the mortgage until it's sold. I don't like that. With a multi-family property, *your tenants* pay your mortgage and expenses until you sell it. That, I like.

OPTION 2: BUY AND HOLD

If you get past that phase where all you can think about is a wad of fast cash, then the next goal is to generate cash every month. That's what I mentioned in the last chapter, when I focused on getting those monthly bills covered by my apartment cash flow. At that stage, your strategy should be to buy and hold.

Use this strategy when you feel that the fundamentals in the market are changing in your favor. If you think you can create additional value in the property through market appreciation, then hold it for a while (usually one to five years).

There must be certain factors present in the market (like impressive job growth) that will create additional demand for properties.

This is the essence of the emerging-market strategy I detail in my book, *Emerging Real Estate Markets*.

While you're holding the property, you'll run it like a business. A qualified property management company will run the property. You'll check financial and operational performance every month. If your management company is doing a good job, you'll also cash checks every month!

While you're holding the property, it's important that you are always raising rents. We call this *pushing rents*. If you're in the right market at the right time, rents should be rising. Every time you rent a vacant unit or do a lease renewal, raise the rents to whatever the market will bear.

Doing this will increase your net operating income. That, in turn, will increase the value of your property. If you are disciplined at this, you will see your equity increase very rapidly.

Know what the best part is? *You* are not raising rents; it's your manager who's doing it!

At some point, it will be time to sell the property and trade up to a bigger property in that market, or something in another emerging market.

Here is an example of this strategy in action:

I bought a 32-unit property in Huntsville, Alabama, for $614,000. At the time, Huntsville was an emerging market. I held the property for 18 months and resold it for $1,100,000. After all costs, the profit was close to $430,000.

I could have assigned that deal to another investor for a quick $20,000. But I liked the market and the deal, so I decided to hold out for the big reward.

Of course, I had a property manager run the building. I would get my profit-and-loss statement every month, along with a cash flow check. I'd occasionally fly down to Huntsville and do a surprise check on my property. (Huntsville's a great city, by the way. Very relaxing, nice people, and a great place to do business.)

I'd find miscellaneous things that I wanted changed, but overall, the property manager was keeping the place nice and maximizing my net operating income, so I was happy!

I took that money and flipped it into a 70-unit complex in Huntsville. I paid $1.6 million for it. Of course, I took no money out of my pocket; I used all the proceeds from the other property to do it. Now I get bigger cash flow and more appreciation. As I write this, I plan on holding that property for about 18 months and expect it to sell for $2.2 million. Then I'll take the $800,000 in total profits and buy a property for $4 million, again with no money out of my pocket. You can do this, too!

It's all about turning your small properties into big properties, and your big properties into bigger properties!

Option 3: Buy, Reposition, and Sell

After your investing has built a solid financial foundation for you, you'll want to make some *real* money. If you're willing to do the work it takes, then you should buy, reposition, and sell.

Repositioning is when you buy a property with a problem, fix that problem, and resell the property for a big profit.

You cannot only reposition a *property*, but also the *tenant base*.

When you reposition, you add value. When talking with brokers, ask them if they have any *value add* deals. They'll know exactly what you mean; they'll also know by that code word that you're a player!

You can add value by raising rents, raising occupancy, doing repairs, increasing income, decreasing expenses, and many other ways.

To reposition the tenant base, you change tenants over time to a profile that is best suited for the property.

Let's say you have a 20-unit apartment building that was built 30 years ago. Because of its age, let's say it's a C property.

Occupancy has dropped to 77 percent and rents are low. They're doing anything they can to keep the old tenants, so they are not raising rents.

That's causing a lot of deferred maintenance on the property (that is, repairs that need to be done and have been neglected). It's hard to get new tenants to move in because the place doesn't look good.

You can see, of course, the *vicious cycle:* Because they can't get new tenants to move in, they don't have the cash to do repairs. Their vacancy drops even more. This is the situation at a lot of properties in need of help.

You look at the deal and realize that the property actually sits in a good B area. You decide you want to take a crack at repositioning it for big profits.

The property is selling for $550,000 and you think you can resell it for $950,000 when you're done. Here is your strategy:

You'll need to repair the interior and exterior of the property. You won't break the bank on the quality of the work, but will install fixtures and appliances that a B tenant would expect to find. Hence, you are repositioning this C property to a B and shooting to reposition the tenant base from a C tenant to a B tenant.

You follow a well-tested process to reposition with the greatest profit. First, you repair the exterior, the common areas (recreation hall, patio, and so forth), and change the name of the property, adding new signage.

For a repositioning to be successful, you must first *change the perception* of the property in the eyes of both the current tenant base and the community.

By changing the appearance of the outside of the property, you've taken the first highly visible step to changing that perception.

You also put up big banners that say *Under New Management*, and *New Management, New Attitude.*

You do not raise rents or market the property for new occupants at this point. If you did, you'd get the same class of tenants that you have in there right now. If you tried to raise rents, you would not attract your new target tenant profile. They're not ready to live in that property until the perception of it has been successfully changed.

The strategy is to keep the current tenants paying rent as long as possible, because you need this money for cash flow. But you realize that only 20 percent to 30 percent will still be living in the property one year from the day you start.

This doesn't mean you will *lose* 70 percent to 80 percent of your occupancy; instead, you'll be *trading up* your tenants. The old tenant profile will move out, and the new profile will move in.

You can count on about 30 percent of your tenant base moving out when this process is over, for one reason or another. Just work it into your figures.

Repositions fail for two reasons:

1. The buyer runs out of money; or
2. The buyer hires the wrong management company.

When you are buying a property to reposition it, you'll need some money behind you. It will see you through the early days, and get you to breakeven and then to positive cash flow.

When doing your calculations, first determine how much the repairs will cost. Then determine what your breakeven occupancy is.

Do this by taking the total amount of expenses you have on the property, including your debt service (that is, the mortgage). Then calculate your average market rent and divide the average rent by your total expenses. That's your breakeven annual rent. Divide that number by 12 and you are now looking at your monthly breakeven rent.

Let's say you have a 30-unit building and your annual expenses, including debt service, is $175,000. Divide that number by 12 to get a monthly expense figure of $14,583. Now divide the $14,583 by the average monthly rent ($650) and you get 22.4. Round that up to 23. This means if you rent 23 units, you will be at breakeven.

To find out what percent occupancy this represents, simply divide the breakeven number needed by the total number of units: 23/30 = .766. This means you need to get to 77 percent occupancy to break even. Occupancy above that will generate positive cash flow.

Now let's say you're buying this building at 65 percent occupancy. You need to figure out how long it will take you to repair the property so you can start leasing it up. Then figure how many units you can lease per month.

At 65 percent occupancy, this means you have about 20 units rented. To get to your 23-unit breakeven number, you'll have to rent an additional three units.

This should not be too difficult. But let's say you're going after bigger fish: Let's add a *zero* to the number of units.

Now you're buying a 300-unit property. Your breakeven is 230 units. If you are buying it at 65 percent then you have 200 units occupied. You must now lease up 30 units.

You must figure out how many units you can lease up each month. Let's say that number works out to be five. If you need 30 units rented, it's going to take you a minimum of six months to get there (30 divided by 5). Now add on how long it will take you to do the repairs and change the perception. Finally, add a couple of more months. (How often do things go perfectly?)

You need six months to lease up, three months to do repairs, and a *fudge factor* of three months. That's a whole year before you get to break even. The question is, do you have enough money to cover expenses for that year until you get there?

Repositions can be cash cows when investors go in with their eyes open and a realistic reserve. They can be disasters when they blunder in without doing the math.

One more thing: How often does a rehab come in at or below budget? So add at least another 10 percent to the cost of your rehab. By doing all of this, you will set yourself up for success.

Let's talk about the other common mistake when repositioning: Hiring the wrong management company. If you hired yourself to manage the property, you just hired the wrong outfit!

When hiring a management company, make sure it has done at least five prior repositioning deals before doing yours. If it hasn't, your project will come in over budget and over deadline. How do you suppose I know this? See that scar right . . . *there?*

Ask the management company what it will do on a regular basis to earn their fee. What they *should* tell you is they walk the property every morning with the contractor. They review the work that was completed the day before, determine what was done right and wrong, and build the plan for the day.

If they don't spontaneously say this, go to the next company.

The manager is responsible for keeping the contractor on the site, doing the work, and doing it right. They should have a checklist, and a *completed* list that is reviewed daily.

For this service, the management company will be paid an extra fee that's 5 percent to 10 percent of the cost of the total construction.

Make sure there are no *overages* (add-ons). Management companies typically get paid 5 percent to 10 percent of all overages as well. They won't have a problem with the contractor's excuse of having to get more money from you, because they benefit, too. You'd better act very upset if people even mention an overage, so they know not to ask for another one.

There are times when you will have to pay an overage. It's usually when a job is started but there was no prior way to know the total extent of work needed until something is opened (usually a wall, the ground, or the roof).

To protect yourself from these situations, when you're getting contractor bids, have them give you price scenarios of different things that might be found when something is opened, and how much each will cost you.

The price will be a lot lower at the time of bidding than if the contractor is already on the job and you discuss price. At that point, you are negotiating from weakness.

I made a fortune repositioning small three- to six-unit apartments in Brockton, Massachusetts. I was buying properties for $100,000 to

$150,000, doing $20,000 to $30,000 worth of repairs, and reselling for $30,000 to $100,000 in profits.

I got very good at doing them and did quite a few. After four years, I graduated to the next level. I went after bigger, 40- to 100-unit properties for much larger profits. I didn't go after larger ones sooner because I was scared! Plus, there was no one out there explaining how to do it, as I'm doing for you right now.

Not long ago, we bought a 192-unit property from a bank for $2.3 million. The bank originally had a mortgage on it for $4.3 million. The process of buying a property below the mortgage value is called *short selling*, which is what we did.

We put $850,000 into it and repositioned the tenant base. This took 18 months. We resold it for $5.6 million and made $2.1 million. It took four months to sell.

In less than two years, we made $2.1 million on a property in Texas that we oversaw from our offices in Rockland, Massachusetts.

This opportunity is not just open to seasoned investors like me. It's open to you, once you know the step-by-step process for repositioning a deal.

Students come to my repositioning boot camp, and get three full days on how to go out and do this same process. What I always find amazing is how these people come from all walks of life: I'm talking different races, all sorts of occupations, and people from all types of cities.

I actually had two 13-year-olds (one from Michigan and another from Canada) who, along with their families, are getting into their first repositioning deal! A grandmother has done *three* of these multi-million-dollar deals! Her name is Esther Bass, from San Francisco. I also have lots of people slaving away at jobs, who are simply looking for a way out of the rat race.

As you go through this book, it gets better: I discuss how to do these deals with no money out of your pocket. I reintroduce Esther in a later chapter, because that's exactly how she did it.

When you get good at these systems, you'll actually be doing all three at the same time. Then you start creating wealth so quickly, you better watch out for whiplash.

You will have become a *transaction engineer.* You'll start to recognize that different properties are good for different strategies. A deal might not be in a great area, but the numbers are good: You'll flip it to another investor and make a nice slug of money.

One of your marketing techniques uncovers another property in a better part of the city. The numbers are just as good, but you decide to keep that one in your portfolio. It has a good chance of appreciating rapidly, is a stable cash generator, and has a good tenant base.

Then someone brings you a property that's in trouble. This time it's mismanagement. You'll look at the numbers and run them through some analysis tools. If you think you can solve the puzzle, you buy it.

Then you fix the problem, increase the cash flow, and increase the quality of the tenant base. As soon as you get it stabilized, you sell it for a big profit.

Your ability to match properties to these investment strategies can make you wealthy beyond your fondest fantasies.

Because repositioning is by far the most time-consuming—and most profitable—approach, I'm devoting the rest of this book to showing you how to do them.

IN THE NEXT CHAPTER

So where are these great deals hiding, anyway?

Right under your nose. The trouble is, most people couldn't recognize a repositioning deal if it walked up and slapped them in the face. All they see is just another plain (or run-down) apartment complex.

In the next chapter, I outfit you with the kind of radar you need to sweep through an area and have these deals jump out at you.

CHAPTER 4

WHERE TO FIND ENORMOUS PROFITS FROM REPOSITIONING

Real estate professionals talk about *highest and best use*. For instance, owning a parking lot in Manhattan might make you a few bucks, but putting a skyscraper on it would be its highest and best use, and could earn you far more money.

Well, *your* highest and best use might be to reposition properties. Stated another way, there are few things you can do as a real estate investor that will earn you more money than to reposition multi-family properties.

The primary goal of repositioning is to enhance the asset and create value. Because multi-family properties produce income, we create value by increasing net operating income.

I talk more about net operating income and analysis in Chapter 7. But let's have a brief discussion of how value is created.

You calculate net operating income (NOI) first by taking property income and subtracting expenses. Do not include the mortgage in this calculation; it will come into play later.

Income:	$150,000
Less Expenses:	– $ 80,000
=NOI:	$ 70,000

This is how much money the property is throwing off, not counting financing. It's important to look at these before-financing numbers because they tell us how the property is doing, regardless of how the owner paid for the property. Some owners will have no financing, and others will.

Back to our example: Is $70,000 a good number? Well, it depends. If we're talking the NOI of a small apartment complex, it's a fabulous number. But if we're clearing 70 grand a year from a giant regional mall, it's a terrible number. Why?

NOI is good or bad only when compared to something, and that something is *property value*. This brings us to a very critical calculation in real estate investing:

$$\text{Capitalization Rate} = \frac{\text{NOI}}{\text{Property Value}}$$

The capitalization rate *(cap rate)* is the return that you would expect to get on your investment if you did not have a mortgage. This is called an *unlevered* or *unleveraged return.*

Cap rates typically run between 6 percent and 12 percent. If a property has a low cap rate, you're getting a lower return compared with the cost of that property.

Why would you accept that? One reason is if the property is very stable and therefore less risky. Just as government bonds can pay a lower interest rate because there's so little risk involved, income properties follow the same principle.

All else being equal, the less risk that an asset carries, the lower its cap rate.

Let's say that we're looking at a B-grade property. B cap rates, depending on the market, range from 7 percent to 8 percent. Let's use 8 percent.

To determine the value of the property, we just use a variation of the preceding equation:

$$\text{Property Value} = \frac{\text{NOI}}{\text{Capitalization Rate}}$$

Just take $70,000 and divide it by 8 percent, or .08. The value of the property is $875,000.

Now we're getting to the real core of the repositioning process:

When you increase your NOI, you increase the property value very quickly.

There are many different things you can do to increase the NOI. Taking just one tool, let's say you raise rents, and increase the NOI from $70,000 to $95,000.

Same property, but now with a higher NOI. To determine your new value, you take that new NOI and divide by 8 percent. $95,000 divided by .08 = $1,187,500!

Raising rents by $25,000 just increased the value of the property by $312,500! Ain't repositioning great?

This may take you only a couple of months to do. Maybe because of not many leases expiring, it could take longer. But regardless of the time it takes, is it hard to do?

No! All you did was raise the rents. And to be accurate about it, *you* didn't even do that! You had your management company do it *for you!* That's an example of a nice, clean repositioning.

Oh, I can hear the naysayers now: *But Dave, it's not that easy to raise rents!*

My response? It is that easy when one of your key screens for buying properties is artificially low rents. Sure, if you inherited a property, you make do with what you have. But if your marketing systems are continually bringing you deals, you get to pick the ones with the greatest increased-profit potential.

IT'S ALL ABOUT RAISING THE NOI

Some people specialize in just buying properties with low rents, raising the rents, and then reselling quickly. That's their niche. That's fine, and it can even make you a lot of money. But if that's all you're doing, you are passing up many lucrative deals!

Sometimes your best bet is to do some repairs. Other times, you need to change the tenant base, as I described in the previous chapter. Still other properties have low occupancy, and your NOI will increase when that challenge is solved.

When purchasing a property to reposition it, you're looking to do one or more of three things. I call them *NOI Factors*, because they all have to do with NOI:

1. NOI Factor 1: Increase the *quantity* of the income stream. This is usually through raising rents, increasing the occupancy, or both.
2. NOI Factor 2: Increase the *quality* of the income stream. When you have tenant turnover, are you able to put in a better quality, more stable tenant than the one who left?
3. NOI Factor 3: Increase the *durability* of the income stream. This has to do with keeping your desirable tenants as long as possible, or releasing quickly when tenants do leave.

We just talked about the effect that a small increase in income has on the property value. When you put more than one of these NOI factors into play at your property, stand back because its value is about to explode.

Later in this book, I talk in much more detail about how to boost these three factors. But first, you need to know exactly what you're looking for when scanning properties for possible repositioning.

PROBLEMS TO LOOK FOR

You'll be on the lookout for specific problems when evaluating a property for repositioning. If you cannot find and then fix one of these problems, don't do the deal.

Wear and Tear

In addition to normal wear, deferred maintenance is an important factor. With the help of a property inspector, you'll evaluate this wear and determine how much it will cost you to fix it. Deferred maintenance is a hidden profit magnifier if you can fix it and still be profitable.

The older the building and the less it's been maintained, the more work will be needed to get it up to snuff.

You should also realize that the older the property, the more maintenance you will *continue to do* after you buy it. All properties are in a constant state of decline, but older properties simply decline faster.

In older properties, you can expect to repair or replace:

- Rotting wood
- Carpets
- Appliances
- Heating and air conditioning
- Sinks, counters, faucets, and pipes (especially underground pipes)

I could go on.

Here's a rule of thumb: If you want to reposition a building that's more than 35 years old, you may be better off reselling as soon as the repairs are done. At that point, the property will look its best. If you keep it in your portfolio, you will constantly be spending money on issues that pop up. (How do you suppose I know this?)

Functional Obsolescence

I'm referring to properties with an outdated design or style. It's also a property that does not have many amenities.

I once looked at a property in Montgomery, Alabama, that was 60 units. It was a good deal in the sense that the property was selling at a much lower price than its market value.

Upon close inspection, it was selling for less than market because the property did not have any air conditioning.

If you're from anywhere near Alabama, you know Montgomery gets *hot!* Without air conditioning, you'll lose many tenants in the late spring and summer months.

The property was made out of brick and had small windows. People don't like to have window air conditioning units if they can help it. However, this was the only alternative for the property because it was built in the early 1950s.

Why had this property been vacant for several *years?* Because all of the competition in the area had bitten the bullet and installed air conditioning.

It's hard to compete when you have such a large disadvantage. Your tenant base then becomes those people who can't afford anything else. And even then, you must keep your rents low to maintain occupancy.

My simple decision was whether I could economically put in central air conditioning and still make a profit on the building. Because it was made of all brick, the answer to that question was *no*.

That was okay, because my marketing system would soon be delivering more deals to me, as your system will for you, too.

MAKING A CHANGE

Let's say you found a property that has one of these problems, and they look like they're fixable. There are two types of changes you can make when repositioning a property: *perceived* and *physical*.

When you are making a physical change, you do just that to the property, whether it's repairs, upgrades, or whatever.

These changes should be done in a certain order: Start with the outside and work your way in.

On the exterior, you may need to fix the roofs, repair woodwork, and replace siding or windows. While you're doing that, you can be working on the landscaping.

Remember, smart investors do not do this work themselves. You should hire a crew instead. The best part about hiring different crews is they can often be working at the same time.

So while roofers do their thing, the painters are hard at work on the outside. Carpenters can be fixing the decks while landscapers improve the grounds.

Don't forget parking lot repairs and tenant mailboxes! Tenants see these every single day. And every single day they affect the tenants' attitude about living in your property.

If your parking lot needs repair, resurfacing, or restriping, get it done. If mailboxes are rusty, rickety, or not all the same, then get new ones as soon as possible. Also make sure the mailbox area is well lit and freshly painted.

If the mailboxes are outside, try to get them out of the weather. On a three-family property where mailboxes are against the side of the building, this may be a little difficult; but see what you can do.

On a 100-unit complex where all mailboxes are in the same place, if the area doesn't have a roof, you need to build one. If you don't have a roof structure over your mailboxes, your tenants will have a negative experience every time it rains and will probably gripe to all the other tenants standing there and getting soaked.

Sure, these are small nuisances. But if tenants who are already annoyed by the mailbox situation then hit a pothole in your parking lot, it can be just the thing to swear to themselves that they're getting *outta there*.

Make living in your property a pleasant experience. From the moment a prospective tenant drives up to the property for the first time, and every day thereafter, you want your property to generate a positive and inviting subconscious feeling.

It should be visually pleasing. That means the exterior of the buildings are in good shape, the landscaping is crisp and plentiful, and the yard is clean.

After focusing on the exterior, now start repairing the common areas. These are all the spaces tenants share, like the basement, recreational areas, hallways, storage areas, and laundry.

The laundry merits careful attention. Tenants can either have good experiences or a constant annoyance that leads to complaints, vandalism, and move-outs.

Laundry areas should be kept well-lit and clean at all times. That usually means daily attention, because things can deteriorate in an ignored laundry area pretty quickly.

The laundry area is considered an amenity. It's supposed to be an additional bonus for living on this property. If it's not kept clean, it becomes a liability.

After focusing on the common areas, now start repairing the units, both vacant and occupied. I'll tell you later my effective strategy that involves repairing units and raising rents. When done right, you'll be goosing that NOI while experiencing very few, if any, tenant move-outs.

THEN THERE'S THE PERCEPTION

The second type of change is the *perceived*. I've already talked about perceived change in the preceding section. These changes have little to do with physical overhauls, and everything to do with how both tenants and the community view the property.

When you are repositioning the property, you'll be turning over a number of tenants. It may be that the current tenant profile is just not ideal for your property once it's fixed up.

In most repositioning cases, the property also suffers from low occupancy. In either case, you need new tenants.

Where will you get these tenants? They'll come from the community. In fact, the majority of your tenants will come from a three-mile radius around your property.

That's an important statistic. Let's say you take over a property and reposition it to attract a certain tenant profile. If that tenant profile makes up a small percent of the population within three miles of your property, your chances of success will be low.

When you're considering purchasing a property, the first thing to do is take a look at that three-mile radius. You must determine the demographic profile of the tenants you want after you improve the property. Then that profile must match what's available within three miles of the property.

There will be times that you look at that profile and decide that the repositioning can't be done, because of the nature of the area. Although that's disappointing to discover, this approach will save you a great deal of time, money, and heartache.

When you make all these changes, you're not only attracting lots of attention from tenants, but also from the community. People talk.

Send the Message that Change Is Happening

Repairs will be one major way to change the perception of this property, and management policies will be the other major way.

The first thing you do after making the repairs I listed earlier is to put all tenants on notice. You inform them that a new management company is on the site and that rules will be enforced. You don't say it quite as bluntly as that, of course; you make it sound instead as diplomatic as possible because you don't want to build any walls.

Many owners and managers make the mistake of building walls between themselves and their tenants instead of building a community, which is much more positive and profitable.

When you take too hard a line toward your tenants, and you become perceived as being simply mean, your tenants will respond by paying late, not paying at all, or moving out.

When you are perceived as firm but fair, you will get the respect of your tenants and they will *want* to live in your community. The only group you'll annoy will be the people who were getting away with breaking the rules under the old owner. They will move out and go to some other property that accepts their nonconformist ways.

The first step in enforcing the rules is to get rid of the slow-payers, non-payers, and any criminal element.

When you get these dregs out of your property, you will build community among the remaining tenants. First, it's a community of people who simply follow the rules and pay their rent on time. Soon, it becomes a community of people who actually enjoy living in this property because they feel like they belong.

When people feel like they belong or they are a part of something, they stay. This is your ultimate goal.

You create this atmosphere by keeping the place clean, orderly, and safe. Put in place a tenant retention program that gets them involved. This could simply be a cookout during nice-weather holidays; it's a great way to let tenants get better acquainted with each other.

I've got a couple of apartment complexes where the local Domino's Pizza™ gives us free pizzas every month to throw a party! Why? They want the exclusive right to put flyers on the doors, and I'm happy to allow it. What a great win/win situation:

- The tenants think we bought them pizza.
- Tenants enjoy a great get-together.
- The pizza company gets more business.
- I gain goodwill and potentially better occupancy and rental rates.

You could also have a mixer for Valentine's Day or a best costume contest for Halloween, which is the biggest adult holiday of the year, by the way. Just get creative.

You may wonder what works for small properties. It can be as simple as:

- A decorate-your-front-door contest.
- A community newsletter that's no more than a flyer.
- Giving tenants a bonus for releasing (a coffee maker, a free carpet cleaning, a ceiling fan).

Create an atmosphere of community and your tenants will stay with you.

Soon, you'll see another benefit: In that three-mile radius around your property, a buzz will soon develop. Your property will be the subject of many conversations, all of them good. People will notice that good things are happening and your property will come to mind when someone's asking around for an apartment.

This is the first sign that your repositioning is successful. It's the breakthrough. You had to invest time and money in this property when its reputation was lower; now you're getting the return on that investment when people who fit your new tenant profile begin to rent units.

The next step gets even better: Word of mouth reaches beyond the three-mile radius to the larger community, and you start attracting tenants from all over. This is when you really start to build momentum in both your property and your cash flow.

THE PROPERTY CYCLE

Real estate investing is all about cycles: Every property goes through a cycle, and so does every town and area.

Growth . . . maturity . . . decline: These are three phases that all properties and areas will experience.

Let's first talk about properties. The growth phase is when it is built. A property will never look better than the day it is completed and the first tenant has yet to unpack.

As the property leases up and becomes full, it enters the mature phase. You create that community we just discussed, whether among families or individual tenants.

The growth phase and transition to maturity can happen quickly, and the mature phase can last a very long time. In fact, your goal as an apartment owner is to have the mature phase last throughout your ownership.

During the mature phase, the building is rented up, and tenants pay their rent on time. The manager is able to keep the property looking good, keep tenants happy, and still deliver cash flow. At the same time, the property value is increasing.

Management *must* take care of any maintenance on the property when it comes due. This is critical for three reasons:

1. If you don't take care of it now, it will only become more expensive.
2. Deferred maintenance sends a clear message to tenants. The most desirable ones will leave first. This goes right back to our rule of treating tenants like the gold that they are. If people know you care about them, they'll stay for a long time.
3. The value of your property will drop. If you try to sell your property with a lot of deferred maintenance, one of two things will happen: Either you'll sell it for a discount to adjust for repair costs, or your buyer will look to negotiate a lower price after the property inspection. You lose either way.

Deferred maintenance also makes your property riskier to purchase, and that gets us back to the valuation equation: If you buy a risky property, you should expect to get a higher return. That means the buyer demands a higher cap rate, which forces the value of your property to go down.

For example, let's say I own a property with an NOI of $400,000 a year. It is a B property in a B area. Such a property would normally trade around an 8 cap rate (they're expressed in percentages, so technically it's .08).

Let's look at what the formula tells us for value:

$$\frac{\text{NOI of \$400,000}}{\text{Cap Rate of .08}} = \text{Value of \$5,000,000}$$

Now let's see what happens when the property is viewed by investors as more risky, and thus acceptable only at a cap rate of 9:

$$\frac{\text{NOI of \$400,000}}{\text{Cap Rate of .09}} = \text{Value of \$4,444,444}$$

You lost almost $600,000 in value because you didn't want to spend the relatively few bucks on repairs. Even worse, you also lost your best tenants. Very, very dumb.

Be a smart owner: Do your repairs on a regular basis and you will protect your asset, tenant base, cash flow, and property value!

Here's a good habit to get your maintenance people into: They should greet each new season with a preventive maintenance checklist. This is a somewhat seasonal list of items to be done to prepare for the next season that is coming up.

Back to the discussion of phases: If deferred maintenance starts happening, your property will enter the decline phase.

This is the worst of the three phases, and it usually happens because owners become cheap, or distracted by other investments, or both.

This is a critical point in the ownership of your property. In fact, it's the tipping point: If you don't do something proactive right here, your investment is now at risk.

You will either spend the money to do the repairs and regain tenant confidence; or you'll fall into the vicious cycle that most likely swallowed up the person you bought the property from.

If you show that you don't care, your management people will soon follow suit. And as your good tenants start moving out, they will be replaced by tenants of lesser quality.

Good tenants don't want to live in a place that doesn't look great, but marginal tenants will. Now your tenant base starts to pay rent late or not at all—because they are marginal tenants!

Your revenues drop. You now *must* apply more money to marketing because you need new tenants. You must market more intensively because your closing ratio is getting worse, because of the condition of the property.

As you spend more money on marketing, there is less money available to fix the property. Eventually, you travel far enough down this spiral until you've had enough. You then throw in the towel and put the property on the market. You pray that you can recoup the money you have put into the property. In most cases, you won't.

Then you end up selling your property to someone like me. Because you are reading this book and might go to my live event on repositioning, the chances of this actually happening to *you* is now very low. You'll be on the lookout for these cheap, bumbling owners and their properties. And you'll be the one to realize the big profits that occur when you reposition these properties correctly!

The decline phase typically ranges from one to two years. How long it takes to get a property back up and running properly will depend on the magnitude of that recent decline. A rule of thumb is that the repositioning will take about as long as the decline.

A COMMON REPOSITIONING MISTAKE

Bringing a property to the market too early is a mistake many repositioners make.

You can avoid this mistake by understanding that occupancy will dip for a few months before it gets better.

This happens because at the point of takeover, you'll most likely have many undesirable tenants. They're the slow-payers, non-payers, and criminal elements. When they realize that a new sheriff is in town and that you'll actually enforce the law, they won't want any part of your property.

Keep in mind that they'll try to get away with it at your place for as long as possible, but your tough-but-fair demeanor won't allow it.

They'll go over to the next complex, where—as they say—the *livin' is easy*. You know, it's the type of property that is in a downward spiral, where management is desperate for any new tenant who can fog a mirror.

A lot of new repositioners don't realize this. They believe that occupancy will be at its lowest level when they take over the property.

What's really dangerous is they make the mistake of using this flawed logic as the basis for their financial forecasts.

I was talking to a student during a break at one of my recent events. He told me that before coming to the event, he bought a 240-unit property that was 62 percent occupied.

When he analyzed the numbers, it appeared to be doing a little better than breakeven at that 62 percent level. He figured he would do the repairs, increase occupancy, and have a huge cash cow on his hands.

When I was talking with him, he was struggling because he had lost nearly 20 percent of his tenant base and was surprised. He was now writing lots of checks for the expenses until he got the property back up to breakeven.

Here's the reality: It takes a little time to change the perception in the community. Even if you waved a wand and made all your external and internal improvements in a flash, it wouldn't matter. That's because not enough time has gone by, and not enough people have passed the property and seen the changes.

Word-of-mouth buzz cannot be rushed.

So Mistake #1 is to expect occupancy to go only up. Then novice repositioners make Mistake #2: They get nervous and lower both the rent and the tenant profile they'll accept. They take applications from the same type of tenants they were trying to eradicate.

When you forecast your cash flow on a repositioning deal, expect to lose 15 to 20 percent of the occupancy you have at the time of takeover. Furthermore, expect that around 70 percent of your tenants at the end of one year will be new. If you know your numbers going in and plan for them, you'll have the capital to see you through to the marketing phase.

The Two Main Reasons Why Repositions Fail

We just finished discussing two mistakes repositioners frequently make. But there are two other—and major—reasons why investors leave the repositioning game for good: They run out of money; or they hire the wrong management company.

You need enough cash to see you through the worst-case scenario of a repositioning deal. You must anticipate all the things that could go wrong, and figure that most or all of them *will* go wrong at the same time. Then you must calculate how much cash will get you out of that situation.

Please note that I said you *need enough cash*, but I did not say it has to be *your own* cash. If you don't have that cash, you'll be interested in Chapter 8, where I talk about the many options you have for letting other people fund your deal.

Many repositioners are good at convincing themselves that everything will go right at the same time instead of going wrong. They start licking their chops at their potential profit before they've made it. That leads to getting into deals with very thin safety margins and getting into trouble. I like nice, fat safety margins, and so should you.

Don't get me wrong: Some deals work out as smoothly as when you drive across the city and hit every green light. But that's pretty rare, especially if you are just beginning.

I could have filled this book with all kinds of fluff about how you simply can't fail if you just go out there and follow my methods. I could have given you only the screaming success stories, and left out the tough ones.

That's not my style. You have the right to know exactly what you're getting into. I certainly am here to tell you that repositioning can be astonishingly profitable. But you can do everything right, and still hit some obstacles on your way to profits. Knowing that will keep you from getting into risky deals, and keep you from getting out of the business.

My own mentor was just as honest with me when I did my first repositioning deals. He is one of the reasons I became so successful. Thank you, Mark Shavel.

The second mistake that repositioners make is they hire the wrong management company. You know the old saying: *If you want a job done right, do it yourself.* Well, when it comes to hiring yourself as the management company, you're making a very big mistake!

You're reading this book because you want to get into the repositioning business. You have no experience as a repositioning manager. Even if you had experience with multi-family management, you need different skills to be a great *repositioning* manager.

I go later into more detail about exactly what the management company should be doing, how they should be compensated, and where to find the good ones. But suffice it to say right now that you don't want your management company learning all about repositioning by managing *your* property.

THE CITY CYCLE

Just as properties have cycles, so do cities. They also go through the three phases of growth, maturity, and decline.

We live in a young country. Many of our cities are between 50 and 200 years old. During the growth period of each city, the creation of a *central business district* (also known as CBD) took place. This is the part of town where businesses congregated. They naturally do that because it's easier to attract many customers to one central area instead of making them go all over the place.

It might initially have been a bank and a saloon. Then stores, hotels, lawyers, insurance agents, and barber shops move in.

As the CBD grows, it usually grows in a particular direction away from town. This is called the *path of progress*. Here's the interesting thing: Over the years for that city, the path of progress almost always goes toward that same direction.

For instance, the path of progress in Boston—one of the nation's oldest cities—has always gone toward the west. Of course, sometimes a natural barrier prevents a city from expanding in a particular direction. In the case of Boston, it was a little tough to grow east, into the Atlantic Ocean! (Though we did literally fill in part of the bay with dirt, old cars, and radiators, and we now call it the *Back Bay*.)

It's similar in Chicago, next to Lake Michigan, and Los Angeles, near the Pacific Ocean.

In every real estate cycle, it's the path of progress that starts to revitalize first. Determine the path of progress in your target city, and focus your efforts there for the greatest potential profits.

REVITALIZATION ZONES

Don't confuse the path of progress with *revitalization zones*. These are areas in a city that have been neglected, usually because of a lack of funding. A city may target such an area to bring it up to current standards. To do this, they offer incentives for investors and contractors to renovate properties there. The city may also give incentives and tax breaks for businesses to move in. These methods can often make an area turn around and even thrive.

A good example of this is the Seaport District in Boston. This area was traditionally known as the *Fish Pier*. The fleet of fishing boats would unload their catch each morning to sell at the fish auction. Naturally, the area was full of warehouses and fish processing plants.

My grandmother owned a fish market when I was growing up. In the summer, when school was out, I would get up early on Tuesdays and Thursdays and we'd go to the Fish Pier to pick up her fish.

We're talking about getting up really early, because business at the fish piers started way before dawn. I remember the first time my grandmother, Mabel Bowser, took me in; I was ten years old. We got there about 6:00 A.M. and stopped off at the Pier Grill. It served breakfast, but it was also a bar so the dockworkers could toss back a few after work—at 11:00A.M.!

The patrons were a bunch of characters and they all knew and respected my grandmother. That first morning I ordered scrambled eggs and chocolate milk. I got my eggs and milk—and a shot of whiskey!

One of the guys yelled over, "If he's going to start, you've got to start him right, Mabel!" and they all roared with laughter.

Some years later, the City of Boston determined that the Fish Pier would be the next revitalization zone and renamed the area the *Seaport District.*

Today, you'll still see the fish piers, but most of the warehouses have been replaced by hotels, restaurants, the federal courthouse, a new museum, and the Boston Convention and Exhibition Center. A once-specialized part of the city is now alive with many forms of commerce.

Revitalization areas are great places for investors like you and me to make a lot of money.

To find out where the revitalization areas are in your target city, call the chamber of commerce or the economic development committee in that area. Ask them for a copy of the *Master Plan.* Almost all cities have a master plan that outlines where the city is focusing its resources.

One thing you must know: The fact that a city *has* a master plan does not mean that the city is *following* it. Sometimes, these plans are partly political documents to show progress on paper, which is a lot easier to do than showing it in real life. Other times, the plan is out of date.

To determine whether the city is actually following the master plan, ride by the areas that are targeted for focus and see if any progress is being made. If so, then great. If not, look elsewhere.

And don't play hero and try to be the first investor into a revitalization area. You know the definition of a *pioneer?* He's the guy face down in the mud, with all the arrows in his back.

Anyway, as the years go by, the CBD will grow larger, and more residential properties are built around the CBD.

Sometimes CBDs become antiquated and the real action starts to happen near giant regional malls or lots of small shopping centers (known as *strip malls*, because the stores are all lined up in a strip).

As towns and cities expand, they complete their growth cycle. People migrate into the area and all the infrastructure gets built, such as roads, highways, bridges, police and fire departments, city offices, and so on.

This evolution continues until land gets scarcer or more difficult to build on. When this occurs, the area has now reached the mature phase.

A city is the same as a property: During the mature phase, as long as the city keeps maintaining the infrastructure, the area will stay in the mature phase. The quality of life holds steady, citizens are active in the community, and the infrastructure meets the needs of the citizens.

Then something happens. Money that would normally be used to support the infrastructure begins to be diverted into other growing areas. Because the area has less money to spend on upkeep, less of it is done. The once-proud area starts to look a little worn.

The best residents start to move out because they don't want to live in a threadbare area. Now the value of properties begins to decline. Lower-income people can afford to live in the area, and they do.

Because property values are declining, the tax base also shrinks. This smaller pool of money now can pay for even fewer projects.

As higher-earning residents flee the area, they stop shopping at the local stores. The stores' revenues begin to decrease. They will eventually decrease to the point where the stores will either close their doors or relocate.

I could go on, but you get the picture.

Smart city governments recognize this cycle and do whatever is necessary to prevent or at least shorten it. Unfortunately, governments are often no better than novice investors at recognizing and counteracting this process.

A good example of this is Pittsburgh, Pennsylvania. At one time, this proud steel-manufacturing city had a population of over 700,000. Today, it hovers around 300,000. It has lost more than half of its residents. Sure, part of the problem may have been due to global competition and other giant forces, but it didn't help that many layers of dysfunctional government made it almost impossible to come up with an effective master plan.

Whether we're talking about a giant metropolis or a brand-new real estate investor, it pays to recognize cycles and *pay the piper early*, thus heading off a long, painful decline.

IN THE NEXT CHAPTER

Once you know what to look for, you might find several excellent repositioning opportunities right in your own backyard. But what if you don't find any right away?

You then need to apply my tested and proven techniques for attracting these deals to you, sometimes from great distances. That's what the next chapter is all about.

CHAPTER 5

How to Attract Deals to You with a Minimum of Time and Money

Yes, this chapter will contain specific marketing methods you can use to attract deals. But I don't want to start there. You can know every trick in the book and still not be successful, if you don't also know some principles behind relationship building. Let's cover those principles first.

The real estate business is like any other business. A major key to unlocking success is to get and keep relationships. Successful relationships rely on three principles:

1. Make it easy to do business with you.
2. Do what you say you will do.
3. Don't be a pain in the butt.

Principle #1: Make It Easy to Do Business with You

Making it easy to do business with you is one of the most important things you can do to develop long-term relationships.

When you're doing business with someone, think to yourself: "What can I do to make this transaction go easier for the other person?" Of course, I don't mean simply to cave in and give the other person everything she wants. But I do mean that you should create a reputation by standing out from the crowd.

If you're dealing directly with a seller, give him all the information he needs to know that you are a qualified buyer. This includes contact information of your lender, the source of your down payment, dates and times of all your inspections, and so on.

This also means you should be proactive in notifying the seller when you are satisfied with the due diligence and can sign off on it. You typically have between 30 days and 60 days to do your due diligence on a property. You'll check the seller's financials, get the physical inspections done, and check the legal issues. (Much more on this in Chapter 7.)

Do you think I'm just stating the obvious? I can tell you from experience that many buyers let the due diligence phase expire and they assume the seller will assume they're in the deal.

Professionals don't make so many assumptions. If you want to separate yourself from the pack, notify the seller the day you sign off on the due diligence, and that you're working your way to the closing. The seller will appreciate this simple phone call immensely.

Of course, return phone calls and e-mails as soon as you can, but certainly within the same day.

Be especially easy to do business with real estate brokers, who are also known as the geese that can lay one golden egg after another at your feet. The good brokers are all jaded and cynical about what careless idiots most investors are. You want to be the tiny minority that's a breath of fresh air.

Imagine that a broker just took a listing for a 20-unit complex. The seller says he wants to sell just as soon as possible. He'll take the first qualified buyer that offers a reasonable price.

If you are the broker, whom are you going to call? Will it be the guy who nitpicked you to death on that first—and last—deal you just did together? You know, the one who called you endlessly, renegotiated the contract at every opportunity, and played undecided until the very last moment?

Or will you call the company that put the property under contract, notified you when all inspections were set up, and filled you in on the type of financing it was using? That company also gave you a complete progress update each week, so you could keep the seller informed and happy. Unless the nitpicker is your brother-in-law, you'll be going with the easy guy.

Investors often make another big mistake: They get some negotiating audio CDs and think that they'll be real pro negotiators, slamming the other side for the very best deal possible.

That's really shortsighted. You know what the very best possible deal is? It's leaving some meat in the current deal for the broker, so that he gives you the *next* great deal that comes along.

My investment company, The Lindahl Group, does a great deal of repeat business with real estate brokers and owners throughout the country. It's because they know when they get into a transaction with us, it will definitely be easy.

PRINCIPLE #2: DO WHAT YOU SAY YOU WILL DO

Sounds awfully obvious. Unfortunately, what's common *sense* is rarely common *practice.*

Did you say that you'd make an offer on the property by the end of the day? Then do it. If you don't, the seller or broker will wonder if you're interested in the deal.

You will be on their mind, occupying space in their head. But it's not free space. They need that space to focus on their business, which is doing more deals. Now they have *dead weight* clogging up that space, in the form of your indecision.

If you get in their mind in the first place, make sure you turn that space into positive thoughts.

When you do this, you'll get the rare reputation of a *performer*—a person whose word actually means something.

Think about it in your own life, and make two mental buckets. Put all the *performers* in one bucket (a teacup is all you need)—and then reserve a landfill-sized dumping ground for all the talkers, wannabes, excuse-givers, and losers who occupy the other bucket.

Do you see why I'm not focusing first on cool marketing techniques for attracting deals? It's because you can absolutely blow away the competition by first taking these few steps to becoming a dependable—and rich—professional.

PRINCIPLE #3: DON'T BE A PAIN IN THE BUTT

Nobody wants to deal with 'em. Life is too short and the list of these people is already longer than your arm.

How do I define *pain in the butt?* It's people who constantly call for little reasons, or always look for ways to get a slightly better deal for themselves.

Sure, get the very best deal possible. But after the negotiation phase is over and you've shaken hands, *do the deal.* This is a very rare practice, and it's also the mark of a professional.

Of course, you should renegotiate when a major unknown problem comes up during the property inspection. These items include bad roofs, boiler problems, erosion problems, and so on. They will cost some serious money to fix.

Do not ask for a lower price just because the kitchen cabinets in Unit 101 are missing two doors. We have a name for you if you do: You've become a *retrader.*

As I mentioned earlier, brokers despise retraders. Why? How would you like to be the one who must now go back to the sellers and ask them to accept less money for a deal that was negotiated several weeks ago?

It wastes both the broker's and the seller's time. Sometimes the seller will simply decline the retrade and walk away from the deal *without giving the buyer the chance to take the original deal.*

If this happens, the broker is out his commission, and your reputation has just turned to dirt. When you retrade, you put the broker's commission in jeopardy.

And get this: The better the deal you have, the more likely that the seller will blow you off and take that deal to someone else. So by all means feel free to renegotiate, but only when it really makes a difference in the big-picture numbers.

The multi-family world becomes small once you get involved. I know we live in a huge country with countless investors and properties. But you won't invest in America; you invest instead in a town somewhere. Maybe it's a subsection of a big city, which is really the same as a town. And the movers and shakers in that town can be counted on one or two hands. You definitely don't have to take your socks off to count them.

These three simple rules are the foundation for the very best, most profitable marketing you can ever do. Now let's talk about the marketing structure you'll build on top of that solid foundation.

INEXPENSIVE DEAL-ATTRACTION TECHNIQUES

Have you ever played around with a pair of binoculars? If you turn them backward and look through the wide end, everything appears tiny and far away, surrounded by a big field of black.

That's how most real estate investors start out. They only see classified ads, or maybe *bandit signs* on telephone poles. To make matters worse, they talk with their friends and relatives, who agree that these methods *don't work*. (Those are the friends and relatives who are usually 9-to-5 slaves, and who never made any money in real estate. Avoid discussing real estate with them.)

When I look at a town, I use the other end of the binoculars. I see amazing detail in the world around me. Everything is crisp and clear. And I notice things most people just pass by.

Let's talk about the very biggest opportunities you'll see when you look at your town through the right end of your own binoculars.

Real Estate Brokers: Your Walking Gold Mines

Just like the switchboard operators in the old days, real estate brokers know intimately everything that's going on in your town, at least as far as real estate is concerned.

The good ones have spent years cultivating their own networks of informants. I shudder to think at the number of doughnuts they've bought and coffee they've drunk while talking to barbers, teachers, lawyers, and business owners.

Brokers dominate the real estate market, because few sellers know of other ways to get rid of their properties.

It will cost you no money to pick up the phone, call a broker, and start to establish a relationship. Notice I said *start to establish* a relationship. If you think you'll call brokers out of the blue and ask them for a quality deal right off the bat—well, you must be consuming something stronger than coffee.

People with valuable assets to dispense will not do business with you unless they *like you* first and *trust you* second. Brokers are no different.

Fortunately, brokers tend to be very gregarious people. After all, they deal with the public constantly. If they didn't like the public, they would have blown their brains out long ago, or at least found a different profession.

Because they need qualified buyers to sell their listings, if you become qualified, they will like you.

Nevertheless, you need a plan to get past the superficial *like* phase and get to the profitable *deal* phase as quickly as possible. You must build rapport by finding something you have in common with the broker—something you can sincerely talk about and share.

I need to tell you a story. A young salesman wanted to earn his reputation by closing the meanest, gruffest, richest prospect he knew. This businessman had eaten up and spit out countless salespeople before him.

So when the salesman was ushered into Mr. Big's office, he immediately started scanning the walls. The office was huge, and he was searching for something that they had in common. Unfortunately, all the stuff on the walls related to rich activities the salesman had no experience in.

Finally he struck pay dirt! Mr. Big liked football! The young guy had played some ball in college and knew everything there was to know about the current pro teams. So he immediately relaxed, because he now knew his opening line.

He shook hands and said: *Hi, Mr. Big, I'm Joe Smith . . . and I just wanted to tell you how impressed I am with that picture behind you. Wow, you're drinking buddies with the famous network sports announcer, John Madden?*

Mr. Big's hint of a smile suddenly changed as he said: *That's not John Madden—that's my wife.*

Okay, so you might not hit a home run every time, but the principle is still sound.

Let's now assume you like each other. Now start to build trust. That usually comes over time, but there are ways to create instant credibility. In your conversations, try to find out some of the people the broker knows. Getting a testimonial later from someone you both know is a superb technique.

Or try to get someone the broker knows to call that broker and put in a good word for you. Remember, brokers have a huge circle of acquaintances. Keep your eyes and ears open and you may find that common link.

People usually trust the referrals of friends or other business associates. Have you already closed deals? Talk about them. Do you have other successes in life? Talk about them.

Whatever you do, do *not* exaggerate or say anything that is not true. If you do, just forget about the relationship.

You're cultivating a money-yielding crop here, and you can't rush the process. It will take a little time to build enough rapport so that the broker starts to send you deals.

Let me qualify that: You may see some deals right away, but the good ones will take awhile to see. After your initial phone call, the broker will send you crummy deals to see whether you buy them.

Don't take it personally; he's just testing you. He wants to know how much you know.

Are you a sweet-talking amateur with more money than brains? Plenty of these people are around. They happened to be at the right place at the right time in their last deal, and they lucked into a fat profit. Now they think they're tycoons.

They don't last beyond one or two deals. If you're one of those investors, the broker will be happy to do marginal deals with you, until you're burned out.

When those deals that don't make sense are sent to you, think of it as a great opportunity. You've just been invited to give the broker a call and make another positive impression.

Call the broker and thank her for the crappy deal. Of course you won't call it that! You'll thank her, instead, for sending it to you. Then you'll concisely explain why the deal doesn't work for you. Do this by describing the type of numbers you need in order to buy a deal.

What do other investors do? They either take the deals and soon get burned out; or they are offended by the garbage deal and don't reply.

Not only will *you* be building more rapport, but the broker will start to respect you. Then you will ask if she has a deal that more closely matches your parameters. The answer may be no, but—trust me—you're now one step closer to getting that deal.

When they are not sending you deals, you still should contact your brokers on a regular basis. Do not be a pest, always asking: *What else you got?*

To separate yourself from the pack, call your brokers with something of value that they can use with their other relationships. Maybe it's a piece of news you heard, or a web site.

When you give this piece of information, you are now a welcome guest instead of an annoying pest. And because you've given the brokers something of value, the *Law of Reciprocity* kicks in. They're unconsciously uncomfortable unless they do something for you.

What do you want? A good listing, of course. So, you take this opportunity to tack on to your conversation: *By the way, Jane, do you have any listings that might be coming on to the market in the near future?*

This is how it's done.

Your competition will call brokers once or twice and then move on. In my experience, the average number of calls it takes to get a decent deal from a broker is seven.

Remember that it's an average. Sometimes you'll get it on call number 2, and other times it will be call number 12. Keep calling. Persistence pays off.

Get Face to Face

Do this as soon as possible.

If you are investing in your own backyard—and initially, you probably will be—this will be easy. Simply call and invite the broker out to lunch. Everyone likes a free lunch. That means you *grab that check fast and pay!* There is no better way to get to know people than to have their undivided attention while breaking bread.

If you're investing in emerging markets like many of my successful students all around this country, you won't often be face to face with brokers. That's because you don't need to be in that market until you've got a deal under agreement. Therefore, all of your rapport-building will be done over the phone. It takes a little longer, but it does work.

When you do get something under contract in a market and visit for the property inspection, plan to spend an extra day or two to meet all the brokers you've been talking to on the phone. Also go to see as many properties as you can, both on the market and off the market.

Don't forget to tell all those brokers about the property you have under contract! Nothing breeds success like success. As soon as you do your first deal in a market, you change from the ugly duckling to the swan. Everyone will know your name, and you'll be considered a performer. Soon, you'll see even more—and better—deals.

Remember what I discussed earlier about ways to get instant credibility? Another way you can become a *performer* without doing your own first deal is to be part of someone else's deals.

I partner with my students all across the country. Because I control more than $140 million—and growing fast—I often have opportunities to let my students in on my own deals. In addition to whatever economic benefits those deals might potentially bring, all my partners can now go out into the real estate community and say that they've closed a deal.

Do they tell them that they technically partnered in the deal with me? I'm guessing not always. Should they? Not necessarily. They're still an owner in a deal, just as if they were a silent money partner in a baseball franchise.

The other great benefit of partnering in deals—whether mine or other people's—is that you're privy to all the inside information and procedures necessary to run an apartment complex. If you are interested in finding out more about this option, just go to www.confidentialinvestments.com and click on the investor application link on the left-hand side of the page.

Brokers and the Market Cycle

Part of your luck in cultivating brokers will depend on which part of a real estate cycle your market is in.

When a market is popular and hot, it's difficult to get consistent, good deals from brokers, unless you're really at the top of their list. They've got all kinds of frantic buyers in the market, and it's their job to get their sellers the highest price possible. After all, higher prices mean higher commissions. Brokers therefore don't care about just relationships; they sometimes put properties out on the open market, where lots of *dumb money* will fight for the deal.

Brokers also tend to list properties aggressively in the later stages of an emerging market. They are typically in competition with other brokers for the listing and if they can show the sellers that they can get a higher price for the property, they will usually get the listing.

Brokers are a great source of business in the down cycle and when the market starts to get better. This, by the way, is when you want to be buying!

Smart investors look for signs that indicate a market will soon be turning upward again. The first sure sign is when it is announced that jobs are coming into an area. I don't mean just that a company hires a few more people; I mean when several companies move into an area, or existing companies significantly expand.

At this stage, brokers have excess inventory on the market and not many buyers. It's a great time to establish relationships with them.

Go Directly to the Owners

You don't always have to work through an intermediary. You can get one great deal after another from even just one multi-family property owner.

Unlike most homeowners, multi-family owners tend to own many properties. (I guess this makes them *multi multi-family owners!*) Some specialize in owning smaller properties, others like just the larger ones, and still others don't care, as long as they're good deals.

Let's say you close on a deal with an owner and you've made it easy to do business with you, done what you say you would do, and weren't a pain in the butt. There's now an excellent chance that the owner will have another property to sell you at some point, and sometimes right away.

One example is a student of mine from Manhattan: Stephane Fymat. He sent out a letter campaign to owners of properties in emerging markets in the Midwest.

He received a call from a gentleman with a 147-unit property for sale in Fort Smith, Arkansas. Stephane analyzed the numbers, negotiated an offer, did his due diligence, and closed on the property.

Once he closed, the owner immediately offered him another property. Notice that the owner did not offer it early on, or even right before the first closing. He waited to see the entire transaction, and then offered another deal.

The owner wanted to make *sure* that Stephane would perform on that first property. After he did, the doors opened wide.

The most important deal you can do is that first one, whether it be with a broker or directly with an owner.

The Number-One way to get deals from owners is from direct mail campaigns. You need to set up a system to contact the owners by mailing to them regularly. You never know when an owner will be ready to sell one of his properties.

One moment an owner may think he'll never sell a property, and then life happens. Something good or bad occurs, and it changes everything. If you're regularly mailing to that owner, you'll have a better chance of being the letter he opens soon after he decided to entertain the idea of selling the property. There is a saying in real estate investing: *Time and circumstances change all sellers' minds.*

The first step in your mailing system is to get a list of property owners. You hire a list broker to do this, or you can get it directly from a city. Just go to City Hall and the assessor's office will most likely have it.

Sometimes, you can get the list on a computer spreadsheet, which is great. You can then sort it any which way you want. Other times, they'll make you pay per copied page. Yet other towns require you to hand-write the names down from their dusty books. Do what you have to do to get those names.

You might want to focus first on all the two-family to four-family owners. They're sometimes a bit less intimidating than the larger properties. I have to tell you, though, that it's the same work to do a larger deal and a smaller one. The point is to *start where you are most comfortable.*

I spent the first several years of my investing career doing mostly two-family to four-family deals.

Another excellent practice is to focus on out-of-state owners. This list usually gets a higher response rate than the others, because they're contacted less by investors.

Out-of-state ownership poses several challenges for investors who are not properly trained. Some believe they are in the landlord business and try to manage the property themselves from a distance. This usually results in disaster.

Others have the brains to hire a management company, but they don't know how to hire the good ones. That's merely a slower disaster.

Your target market, therefore, should be these burned-out landlords who are investing from out of town in your town. In other words, their properties are right in your backyard, but these investors are struggling with them.

I discuss later where to get good management companies and how to oversee them for optimum results.

Set up your letter campaign so that you're mailing at least once a quarter to these owners. Set up a calendar and put it in a place where you'll see it regularly. Mark out your mailing campaign for the entire year so you know which days you'll be mailing to your two-family-to-four-family list and what other days you may mail to your out-of-towners.

If you follow my advice, you're set up for success. If you don't, it probably won't get done.

Here is the most important part of the direct mail process: *Hire someone to do it for you.*

I know, I know: That costs money. I suggest you find that money as soon as you can. It's important, so you stay in the real estate investing business.

If you try to do this job yourself, you may do it once or twice. Then you'll put it off and pretty soon it won't get done. (How do you suppose I discovered this!) In the meantime, some other investor is getting those deals.

Hire a family member, high school kid, disabled vet, disabled other person, the ladies at the elderly center . . . there are plenty of people available to do this simple task for not much money.

Set these people up with the list and their supplies, and let them go to town. Your job is to handle calls from sellers and refresh the list at the start of every year. Be sure to pay your people on time. The fastest way to lose a good producer is to be a slow payer. Paying everyone quickly is a real key to success.

If you can't find anyone local to hire, there are many companies that will do this type of work. Just google *direct mail services* or words to that effect, and you'll have plenty of companies to call. I've been using a company out of Whitman, Massachusetts, called Spectrum Press. They do a great job, their rates are reasonable, and it's always done on time.

Direct mail is going to cost you a little money. But compared to starting other businesses, it's nothing. Fortunately, you can get started by mailing to a list of just 100 owners. As you start doing deals, increase that until you're mailing 1,000 owners a month.

I'm serious: When you are doing that volume, you'll have an endless supply of deals coming into your office. Better yet, you'll be able to cherry-pick the very best ones, because you know the next deal is right around the corner. Also think about how well you'll have your hand on the pulse of that market when you see deal after deal!

My suggestion is that $20,000 should be the minimum profit you build into any deal. In other words, if you can't do it for a 20-grand profit, don't do the deal. I get more into the numbers in a later chapter, but bear with me on the profit target.

(I can't resist adding here that when you do multi-family investing, $20,000 is *chump change*. It's possible to do your very first deal and get a six-figure profit. I had a student in Augusta, Georgia, do just that. Keep reading this book, and your profits from your first repositioning deal can reach six figures, too!)

Okay, so we're being conservative for now and assuming a $20,000 profit from a deal. Let's now look at the marketing costs to attract that deal.

As a rule of thumb, for every 1,000 letters you send out, you'll get a 1 percent response. That 1 percent response will get you 8 to 12 calls from sellers. Several of those calls will be half-interested tire-kickers. One to three of them, however, will be from serious sellers. On average, you'll get one deal to close.

Some months, you will send out 1,000 letters and get *zero* deals. Other months, you'll do two or even three deals.

Keep in mind that you won't need to find 1,000 new potential sellers each month. You'll be mailing second, third, and even seventh letters to people already on your list.

When you're mailing 1,000 letters a month, you're destined for success. Just consider how the vast majority of people are talkers, not doers. That includes your competition. So 75 percent will never mail a single letter. Twenty percent will mail a few dozen letters, and lose interest. The remaining 5 percent may get up to 100 or so letters for a month or two, and then give up. You will be in such a small minority that you're a rounding error! That's right, you don't even rate 1 percent, because you'll have virtually no competition.

The average direct mail piece costs 75 cents to get it out the door. If you're doing 1,000 letters a month, that's going to cost you $750. If that's more than you can afford, then start with what you can afford.

If you multiply that by 12, then in one year, you've spent $9,000 to get your mailings out the door. If you are averaging one deal a month, you're making $20,000 a month. In one month, you've more than paid for your marketing for the whole year!

Of course, there will be a lag time between when you start and when you do your first deal. Therefore, don't buy that yacht quite yet. Just get the brochure.

So after one year of averaging one deal a month, you can make $240,000, all coming from your marketing costs of a lousy $9,000. Do those numbers work for you?

What would happen if you did a 50-unit complex and your profit was $350,000? How many of those would you have to do to live the lifestyle you want? And what would you do with all of your free time?

You would now have *The Attitude!* That means you get to do:

- *What* you want
- *When* you want
- *Where* you want
- For *as long as* you want, and
- *With whom* you want!

Yeah, baby!

Direct mail works in all phases of the market cycle. It's one of the few marketing techniques that do. Direct mail your way to wealth!

OTHER TECHNIQUES THAT COST LITTLE BUT BRING BIG RESULTS

Become a member of your local landlord association. Just about every area has one. At these meetings, you can mingle with other like-minded people. You'll also hear different guest speakers each month.

They'll show you new tips and techniques that you can use to become more profitable.

Don't think you have to be a landlord to be a member of the landlord association. Remember, you will be an investor! Let other people do your landlording and property management. You'll oversee them as an *asset* manager.

Nevertheless, you want to be knowledgeable about landlording, so the people you're managing will realize you know what you're talking about. Knowledge will give you power. No one will be able to pull the wool over your eyes. After all, there are a lot of foxes dressed up in sheep's clothing out there!

The main reason to be a member of the local landlord association is so you can get to know the other owners. These owners will eventually become sellers. If they like and trust you, there's a good chance they will sell their deals to you.

Don't just be a *bump on a log* in these groups. Remember, you want to stand out as an action-taker, and associate with the movers and shakers in the group. Do this by joining committees and boards that are part of the association.

Most of those groups are populated by the key people. They're the more successful ones, who also find time to volunteer. Set yourself apart from the masses by volunteering for projects. Yes, it takes time. Yes, it's boring. Yes, you could be doing more direct mail or making more offers instead of licking envelopes. What you're really doing is—again—setting yourself apart from everyone else, and earning the good favor of the key contacts.

Eventually, you can take on a leadership position. Whether it be president, vice president, or treasurer, become an officer and you will get instant respect and credibility.

What if there is no landlord association in your area? Start one. When I first started investing in Brockton, Massachusetts, there was no landlord association. I got together with a group of other like-minded investors (Carl Schuler, Jodi Beckman, and Faith Frazier: Remember me?) and we started the *Metro South Property Owners Association.*

It's interesting to note that Faith wasn't a property owner, but was president of an organization that provided housing for needy people. She helped start the group so she could network with landlords and get more of her people into apartments. Smart lady.

The first meeting had only a few people, but it grew fast. We had all kinds of great speakers come and talk to us: judges, lead-paint experts, other investors, financing experts, and many others. Whenever I wanted to know something, I'd invite an expert to come speak to us—for free!

The group still meets to this day, nearly 14 years later. I'm proud to be one of the founding members.

GO AFTER THE *DON'T WANTERS*

Show me a group of landlords and I'll bet that at least some of them are thinking of selling their properties. They entertained the thought last year and maybe even the year before. Now they are thinking about it again.

Forget about them. You instead want the landlords that fall into the category of true *Don't Wanters.*

These landlords are fed up and burned out. They've had it, and are ready to sell.

How do landlords become *Don't Wanters?* They're in the landlord business and are not good at it. They despise tenants but have to unclog their toilets on Christmas Day. They let maintenance slip. The bottom line is they never found out what you already know from reading this book: How to find good deals, buy right, and never manage them yourself.

Life should be about family, friends, hobbies, and free time. *Don't Wanters* haven't experienced any of that for a while, and they want it back.

One sure place to find *Don't Wanters* is where the local board of health takes its bad landlords to court. When I say *bad landlords,* I mean landlords who have been served notice that they have a housing violation. It must be rectified within a certain period—usually 30 days—and they don't do it. Now they must appear in court.

If landlords know they must appear before a judge if they don't do repairs, and they still don't do them—well, you're looking at freshly minted *Don't Wanters.*

Here's what you do: Locate that courthouse, which will be either your local district court or housing court. Get the list of owners who are scheduled to appear before the judge. It usually has their names and addresses and is posted on the court date. Most courts hold this type of hearing on the same day of each week.

Start going to a few of these sessions. They're actually quite interesting. Just sit in the back of the courtroom and listen to cases for the day.

One time I went, a tenant pointed to the landlord and said: *Your Honor, that man's a slumlord!*

Without missing a beat, the landlord pointed at the tenant and said: *Your Honor, that woman's a pig!* (She did look like one.)

Some of it is sad. You'll hear stories of people who tried to make it work out, but one thing happened and then another.

You hear stories from angry or defiant people, and from those who've just given up. You'll see this whole rainbow of situations in both the tenants and landlords who show up.

The *Don't Wanters* are easy to spot. You can hear it in their tone of voice. They've had enough and want out.

Follow them out of the courtroom, pull them aside in the hall, and give them your business card. Tell them you specialize in buying their type of property, you may want to buy theirs, and would they be interested in selling. Then just listen to what they have to say.

As with every other deal-attracting technique, you'll go through many *no thanks* responses for every *how soon can we meet* response. That's okay. You just need one good deal to fatten your bank account, big time. Plus this method of finding deals costs zero money and very little time.

CRUISING FOR DOLLARS

Just hop in your car, cruise neighborhoods that you're interested in investing in, and look at all the multi-family properties in the area.

Identify the ones you would be proud to own and proud to show off to your family and friends.

Then look at the ones that aren't so nice. Maybe they need paint, better landscaping, or the roof needs to be fixed. When you see trashy looking properties with broken shades and sheets hung up across windows, think *money*!

These properties were once proud like the ones you'd like to buy, but they have fallen on hard times. The owners don't care about them anymore.

Whatever the case, *you* can make this property better! You can restore it to its former glory. When you make it a proud place to live again, you'll be making some very nice profits at the same time.

You can get many properties for below-market prices, because of the deferred maintenance. If you can't get it for well below market, don't bother. When you see one of these properties, pull over, get out, knock on a door, and ask the tenant if you can have the owner's contact information. You explain that you'd like to do the needed repairs on the property. The tenant's eyes will widen and you'll have the owner's name in a flash.

You're telling the truth, because you'll do those repairs when you buy it!

Maybe the tenants don't know who the owner is (smart owner). In that case, go online or visit the assessor's office. See where the city is sending the tax bill, and give that person a call. If you can't find the number, then do your direct-mail thing.

ANOTHER WAY TO CRUISE

You say you want *yet another* way to find deals? Okay, get on the Internet. Many sites now list commercial properties.

The granddaddy of them all is loopnet.com. This service is nationwide and very popular: commercial brokers, residential brokers selling commercial properties, and lots of investors like you and me are on it constantly.

You'll find all sorts of commercial and multi-family deals on this site. But remember one important fact: Before the properties from commercial brokers go on the site, they have most likely been heavily picked-over.

When commercial brokers get a listing, they try to sell it to their private buyers' list first. (You'll be on that list if you follow my earlier advice.) If these favored buyers don't like it, then it goes to the rest of their list.

If they don't buy it, then the brokers share the deal with everyone in the office, because they at least want the office to survive.

If it's still not sold, it goes onto Loopnet or a similar site. I can now hear you asking: *Well, why then should I waste my time on dog properties, Dave?*

Because you can *still* find good deals on Loopnet! I got a 200-unit building in Austin, Texas, for $8.5 million that was then appraised at $10.5 million.

Sure, it will take a lot of number crunching through crummy deals to find a decent one. You're mining for diamonds, and if you think they're just lying about, you'll never make it in this business. Add Loopnet as just one more way to get exposure to more deals, and you will soon become wealthy.

OH SO MANY WAYS TO GET DEALS

I just covered some of the most productive ways to get a constant flow of deals across your desk. But there are many more ways! You can:

- Go after foreclosures, big and small.
- Go to eviction court.
- Network with estate attorneys.
- Network with accountants.
- Network with financial planners.
- Network with the disposition agents of other real estate companies.
- Talk with real estate investment trusts and see what they might have in their portfolio that they want to dispose of.
- Read the classifieds.
- Put in a classified ad.

DON'T MAKE THESE THREE MISTAKES

Don't get me started on the many ways that investors sabotage their own success. But here are three of the biggies:

1. They sit on their butts and never get started.
2. They actually get started, but give up at the first sign of difficulty or lack of results.

3. They look for the single *Silver-Bullet Technique* that will make them filthy rich, and they never find it, so they give up.

If you want to rely on one single form of marketing to get your deals, just put this book down, sell it on eBay, and go back to your day job.

As my good friend, Jon Rozek, says: I can't tell you one way to get 50 deals, but I can tell you 50 ways to get one deal, and you should be doing all of them!

If you follow that advice, you'll soon blow the doors off your bank account.

All of us first think we're entering the real estate investing business, when the real truth is that we're in the marketing business, and real estate is our product. If you don't get this firmly fixed between your ears, you won't be in business for long.

At my live events, we spend a great deal of time on marketing. Not only do my students become proficient in marketing to get deals, they also leave with complete marketing systems they can plug in when they get home, to get that deal machine humming. If you want more information on these opportunities, just go to MultiFamilyMillions.com and type in the keyword "marketing."

Do not fall into the trap of taking the easy way out, and only surfing the Internet for deals. Yes, they're out there. But what are you waiting for? Do you want to get rich pronto, or just some day in the distant future? If the answer's pronto, then get off your duff, pick up the phone, send some letters, get some lunch appointments, and get out there!

I know it will be out of your comfort zone. It sure was out of mine, at first. But soon two funny things happen:

1. You get used to the marketing, and each action gets easier.
2. You start making money.

There's nothing like sliding that big check across to the bank teller whose eyes widen. It more than makes up for all those dead-end leads you'll follow.

Use many forms of marketing and you'll soon see what I mean. You'll be a hero to your spouse, you'll be the envy of the landlord association, your face will clear up, and you'll have a better sex life!

IN THE NEXT CHAPTER

You've located one or more good repositioning possibilities. Now we must dive in a little deeper to understand the principles behind what we're about to do.

You need to know when you're looking at a mess that's really a wonderful opportunity—and when you're looking at just a mess. I sort them out in the next pages.

CHAPTER 6

SEPARATING THE GOLD MINES FROM THE LAND MINES

Some multi-family properties are indeed like gold mines: You stake your claim, hire workers to do your digging, and enjoy a steady stream of riches from that property.

Unfortunately, ignorant investors can instead get saddled with a big land mine. Is it actually a surprise that the road to apartment wealth would take you through a minefield? After all, if it were possible to simply blunder into investing and make a fortune, everyone would be rich.

You are not one of those investors because you got off your duff and are reading this book. You figured out that the best way to navigate that minefield is to have a guide who's been there many times before. That guide is me.

By following tested and proven methods, you'll save yourself immeasurable suffering and time. Yes, you'll still get beat up a little. I don't want to lie to you and say you'll never experience any difficulties. I'm just saying that you're way ahead of the game by piggybacking on someone who's been there.

THE POWER OF NEGATIVE THINKING

"But Dave, I thought it was the Power of *Positive* Thinking!"

Here's where positive thinking gets investors in trouble: They wait until a market is hot. Then they pay too much to buy a property, rationalizing that they'll sell it to a bigger fool who waited even longer to buy.

Negative thinking goes like this: You buy properties that have problems, preferably in areas that have not yet fully recovered from their cyclical downswings. Your family and friends all swear that you've lost your mind or are on designer drugs. You smile and drink a beer with them, but you don't listen to them.

You know a number of things they don't, and one of them is *how to force a property to appreciate.*

That's right, forced appreciation. When you take a property with a problem, and fix that problem, you can substantially increase the value of the property, regardless of general market trends. This is called a *value play*.

This can be done only if you follow Dave's Golden Rule of Multi-Family Investing: Only buy based on *actual numbers*.

I already went through this, but maybe you were eating a sandwich when I said it before, and I need to hammer it into your head. Do *not* buy any property based on *pro forma* forecasted numbers. If you do, you'll not only blow a lot of cash, but I'll have to hunt you down and slap you around!

PROFITING FROM VALUE PLAYS

How can you hope to profit from a value play, when it's a problem the previous owner couldn't fix? You'll benefit because you're taking the time to discover the types of properties that are not only under-valued, but are fixable.

One of my mentors has a net worth over $500 million. He once told me: "Dave, the reason I am so successful is because I never reach the top of the mountain; I continue to climb little hills." He continues to educate himself.

Your typical value play is different from a flip. The typical flip takes three to six months. A typical value play deal will take 12 to

24 months to turn around, depending on size and complexity of the repositioning.

When I was building my portfolio of three- to six-unit properties in Brockton, it typically took me three to six months to do all the repairs and another couple of months to lease them up. I then either held the property for nice cash flow, or flipped it for a single fat check.

At the other end of the spectrum, as I write this book, I'm at the tail end of a 400-unit repositioning that will have taken almost 24 months to complete. When you put that kind of time in a deal, you should expect a two-comma profit. What's a *two-comma profit?* It's when your number is big enough that it requires two commas to write.

I know that one of your fears with multi-family properties is the fear of big numbers. I had that same fear. It kept me in small properties for almost four years. When I finally got over the fear of doing bigger deals, I couldn't believe how easy they were, and we just kept getting bigger. You, too, can soon be in the same position.

For now, let's assume you are like I was, and you want to do small deals for a while. That's okay: The average profit on my little three-family deals was between $30,000 and $100,000.

Let's look at what some of these hidden gold mines look like.

How to Find—and Profit from—Burned-Out Landlords

They're everywhere, as we discussed earlier, and their properties are easy to spot: Simply look for properties that are run down. You can usually spot multiple problems after just glancing at the property from the street.

This is the same landlord that you will find in housing court. I described that process in the previous chapter. He's a *don't wanter*, and he's advertising it to the world with his poorly maintained property.

How do we find him if he's not at housing court this week? First ask the tenants. They've probably been calling him regularly to complain about all the repairs that are not getting done.

If that doesn't work, go to the neighbors. They've been calling him too, because of the unruly residents. If that doesn't work, go online or go to your local assessor's office and find out where the tax bill is going.

If you can get the phone number, call the owner. Otherwise, get the address and send him a letter saying that you want to buy the property.

PROFITING FROM MANAGEMENT NIGHTMARES

Just because you hire a management company, your worries are not over.

It's true that you've minimized the time it will take to oversee that asset: You won't be dealing with tenants, paying property bills, collecting rent, or repairing the property.

But what you do need to do—and what some investors neglect to do—is manage the manager.

Whether through laziness or sheer incompetence, some managers fall down on the job. Let me count the ways:

1. Inability to keep the property full
2. Inability to collect rents
3. Higher-than-usual expenses
4. Poor tenant screening
5. Higher-than-usual evictions
6. Property not clean
7. Leasing office not attended
8. Poor tenant relations
9. Poor follow-up on tenant requests
10. Slow to get units ready to rent out again
11. Not telling you about expenses
12. Poor landscaping upkeep

The first three items on the list above are the dirtiest of this *dirty dozen list.* They're the mark of a bad manager, and of a soon-to-be-poorer owner.

Bad management companies are very good at one thing: creative excuses. Don't listen to the yarns they spin. Give a property management company three months to perform. If you're not getting the cash flow you were expecting, it's time to give them notice and bring the next manager in.

You should always have a clause in your management agreement that gives you (and the management company) a 30-day option to cancel the contract. Many management companies want you to sign for a one-year term. Don't do it.

Simply write in the 30-day option, initial it, and ask the management company to initial it too. If the company won't agree to this change, then look for another manager.

Also, do not get suckered into the *turning-the-corner* speech. You'll hear how the property is just about to turn that corner and if you only give them another 60 days, you'll see how right they were. Don't do it.

PROPERTIES THAT NEED REPAIR: WHERE THE GOLD IS

One of the best ways to add value to properties is through repairs. Many people shy away from a property because it needs repairs, but the savvy investor loves these properties. Usually the uglier, the better, as long as you buy the property at a discount.

How much of a discount? It depends, of course, on the property and amount of repairs. As a ballpark figure, you should make a 20 percent profit on a property *after* your repair costs are factored in.

The very best kind of run-down properties are those that look awful, but need only cosmetic repairs. Here's what I mean:

Types of Properties to Buy . . . And Avoid

	Looks Nice	**Looks Terrible**
Structural Problems	Danger! These properties ruin amateur investors.	Only for: 1. Very serious renovators; or 2. Dumb investors
Cosmetic Problems	You won't get much of a discount here.	THIS is what you're looking for!

When you're experienced enough, you can consider going after the properties that are truly run down, both in appearance and structure. But even then, the easiest money to be made will be in the properties that look simply awful, but need only skin-deep renovations. You'll be trying to find these deals your whole investing career.

One of my students, Ruth Martinez, saw a six-family property in her city that looked in need of repair. She contacted the real estate broker and discovered the owner was motivated to sell the property. After a little negotiation, she bought it for $374,000.

Her improvements consisted of spiffing up the exterior with landscaping and siding repairs. The bigger challenge was that she didn't have the greatest tenant base.

It seems that the tenants didn't like to pay their rent. Ruth got rid of the slow payers and non-payers. She took the predictable hit with a half-empty building and a couple of difficult months, but soon filled those units with better-quality tenants paying higher rents.

When she sold the building, she made over $200,000 in profit. Congratulations, Ruth!

Cosmetic repairs include minor items such as interior carpets, appliances, and paint. On the exterior, it may include light repairs on woodwork, roofing, and siding.

On a typical cosmetic repositioning, expect to spend on interior and exterior repairs between $1,000 and $4,000 per unit.

Above $4,000, it's becoming a major repair job, and the risk is going up. The more repairs, the more unknowns you may uncover. That means you could end up spending more, taking longer, or both. Plus, income could be affected because rental units must stay empty longer.

Avoid Certain Repairs

Here's the simple rule: *Avoid any repair that does not increase the value of the property.* Almost all cosmetic repairs increase the value of the property, but many expensive structural and environmental repairs do not.

After all, people *assume* that foundations are not crumbling, termites have not feasted for years, and the property is not swimming in gasoline from a nearby gas station. If you're the sad owner of a property with such problems—even sadder if you didn't know these problems going in—you'll have to fix them. But they're not enhancing your curb appeal; they're just getting you back up to zero, so to speak.

Don't think you can just wait a while and pawn the property off on someone else. You are risking the loss of your certificate of occupancy. This means the city will shut down your building and your tenants will be forced to move out on short notice, leaving you with no cash flow and no business.

Environmental repairs are the same. If they appear, you must handle them quickly. Even though they will not add value to the property, you cannot risk someone getting ill from the problem. The city might shut you down for these problems too, depending on the magnitude.

Example: Mold

Another student of mine was under contract for a 14-unit apartment building in an emerging market. The property inspection revealed there was a mold problem in the building. Black mold.

Just because it's black mold doesn't mean it's toxic. A mold specialist can determine what you're dealing with. But the fact that it is mold is a problem. Even when not toxic, mold causes many health problems. (If you ever enter an apartment and see mold growing on the walls, pull your shirt over your mouth and nose to protect your lungs from mold spores entering.)

My student called a mold specialist and discovered it was not toxic. Normally, a mold cleanup is not difficult. You must remove all the drywall and any other material covering the walls, down to the studs. The real problem lies in where the water source is that caused the mold. If it can be isolated and repaired, then you could be back on track.

Sometimes, the water source cannot be isolated and repaired. For instance, a high water table is not economically fixable. If your property inspector found this situation, just pay his inspection bill and move on to the next property.

To finish the story, my student discovered that the mold was fixable, but the water source was not, so he passed on the deal.

SOLVING HIGH-VACANCY PROBLEMS—ONCE AND FOR ALL

High vacancies are one of the easiest problems to cure.

To get new tenants, most landlords follow this process:

1. Put an ad in the classifieds.
2. Put one hand up in front of their face.
3. Put their other hand up, and join it with the first hand.
4. Get on their knees and pray.

This *system* leads to vacancies. That then leads to limited cash flow. Without the cash, repairs are put off. Pretty soon, tenants complain, and then leave.

This is a very nasty downward cycle, because these landlords must now spend more on advertising, while having less cash flow. They finally burn out, and sell the property at a very nice discount to investors like me—and soon, you.

Is it just wishful thinking that the previous landlord could not keep the property full, and we think we can do better? No, it's because we have a tested and proven system for filling those units.

Instead of using the *rifle approach* to shoot only at people who read the classifieds, we will blast our shotgun and hit far more potential renters.

We'll set up a web page and direct people to it. Did you know that almost 30 percent of potential applicants come from the Web?

Then we will do a postcard campaign to people living in buildings like ours and tempt them to move to ours. They have already indicated that they like our building style; now it's up to us to make it more enticing to live at our place than where they currently reside.

We'll contact the human resource managers at all major employers in the area. It's in their best interest to find housing for their employees, so let's make it easy for them to do just that.

And at this point, we're just getting started with the possibilities!

HOW I FILLED 400 UNITS

I bought a property with a group of investors in Huntsville, Alabama. When we purchased the property, it was 60 percent occupied. After three months, it was down to 46 percent. Remember, the slow payers, non-payers, and criminals go first.

To fill that property we did the following:

- Tenant referral program: Current tenants get $100 for referring a new tenant to us.
- Open houses: We invited the community to check out our improvements and enticed them to live there.
- Special for Soldiers: We were near a military base, so this was a natural.
- Banners: We put them up in the entryway to the complex.
- Corporate outreach program (again, through the human resources departments).
- Flyers at the laundromats, hair salons, and nail salons.
- Ads in the local college newspaper.
- Ads in ethnic newspapers.
- Classified ads.
- Strong tenant retention program: Once the good ones are in, we work to *keep* them in.

Not one of these programs was responsible for the majority of leads, but together, they brought in the traffic and allowed us to fill the complex.

Your vacancy rate should be equal to or better than the surrounding area that you are in. If that area is at 90 percent, your complex should also be at least at 90 percent. In this case, you can't expect to get the property quite to 95 percent occupancy because the market is not there yet.

If it happens, great, but here's your warning: *Expect* to get higher occupancy than surrounding properties, but *base your financial projections* on the more conservative average occupancy for the area.

Remember, you can get average occupancy for the area by calling local brokers or property managers you've been cultivating.

Properties with high vacancies are an *opportunity*. Having only one kind of marketing solution is a *problem*.

HOW TO RAISE RENTS AT TAKEOVER AND NOT LOSE YOUR TENANTS

Whenever you take over a property, there will be tenant turnover. People leave for all sorts of reasons:

- They don't know what's going to happen and don't want to stick around to find out.
- They hear rumors.
- They just *know* you'll be raising rents.

Expect it.

Let's assume you're buying a property where rents are low by $100 a month. That's a pretty big jump, and you're concerned the tenants won't accept it and will leave in droves. Yet you bought the property to realize that hidden market value by getting the rents up. Here's how you do it:

Step 1: Be absolutely sure that the increase will bring you to true market rents. Do this by shopping your competition. Simply go over to these different apartment complexes and tell them you are interested in renting. Have them show you around the property and into a unit.

This is done all the time by investors and owners. The competition *expects* to be shopped by you. Sooner or later, it will be done to your management company, too, and that's fine. After you own the property, you should have your property manager shop the competition every month with a phone call, or with a friend making the call.

You must shop the competition in person, to see how their property compares to yours: Where are they strong and weak? How can you make your property better? And—most important—what are they charging? Do this before you close on the property.

Armed with information from four or five of your competitors, you can now determine what your rents should be. After you close on the property, put your plan into action.

Step 2: Get the exterior of the property looking good. Do all repairs, paint the exterior, improve the landscaping, improve the lighting, and restripe or blacktop the parking lot. Whatever you need to do to show the tenants that *times have changed and new ownership has a new attitude*, do it.

Step 3: Repair the common areas, where all tenants move around freely. This includes hallways, basements, pool area, clubhouse, and so on.

Get those areas looking good, even if it costs you. With the exterior shining and the interior common areas now in tip-top shape, it's time for the next step.

Step 4: Audit your rent roll. Determine which leases will expire within the next 30 to 60 days. Have your manager visit these tenants, explain the new, positive things that are happening to the property, and take an inventory of their units.

They then write down any repairs that need to be made, and schedule a time for your maintenance person to come in and do those repairs.

Yes, I know I told you to do an inspection of every unit before buying the property. This is different. This time, we want to know what each tenant thinks should be done. We're on a mission to raise the quality of the property and raise rents, too. This is how we get there.

Step 5: When repairs are complete, your manager visits all tenants again and offers them a bonus to sign a new lease for another year, at the higher market rate. The bonus could be a ceiling fan, carpet shampoo, accent wall—be creative. You're looking for relatively inexpensive items that have high perceived value. Let the tenants suggest ideas. They may come up with bonuses you never thought of, but are within your budget.

These five steps will allow you to keep tenant turnover at a minimum while you significantly increase rents.

How to Raise Rents Steadily While Keeping Your Tenants

The great opportunity to increase the value of your property quickly is to find properties with low rents.

Owners don't raise rents for two reasons:

1. They're afraid if they raise the rents, tenants will ask them to make repairs. They may be right, but it's still bad logic: Raising

rents will increase cash flow and property value. Doing repairs will maintain that value.

2. They're afraid tenants will move out.

In one study I saw, researchers did exit polling to discover the main reasons why tenants moved out. Rising rental rates was number three on the list. Number one was failure to take care of repair requests.

When is it time to raise rents? Any time your property is at 95 percent occupancy or above. There will be very little turnover as long as you raise them just to market levels and you've been treating your tenants fairly.

You should also raise your rents every year, even if the market has *not* gone up. Train your tenants to expect *some* annual rent increase. Perhaps it's only $15 to $20. This is called a *nuisance* increase. It's certainly not enough for a tenant to move out, but it sure does help your numbers!

Come on, Dave, how much could a lousy 20 bucks help me out?

You have a 10-unit building, and you increase rents by $20 per month. Let's see:

10 units times $20 per month = $200 . . . times 12 months = $2,400.

Are you already so filthy rich that you can't think of a thing to do with an extra $2,400?

Plus, it gets better: At a 10 Cap Rate, we divide the $2,400 by .10 to arrive at a property value increase of $24,000.

You just created 24 thousand bucks with a nuisance increase that tenants were probably *relieved* was not higher!

What if you sold that property? The $24,000 will allow you to buy a bigger property on your next purchase. Assuming that you put 20 percent down, you've increased your purchasing power by:

$24,000 divided by .2 = $120,000.

Ain't math great?

Remember my earlier comment: *The faster you go big, the faster you become wealthy.*

Well, if you have a 100-unit apartment building and do a nuisance increase of $20 per month, your cash flow just increased by:

100 units times $20 per month = $2,000 . . . times 12 months = $24,000 per year!

In how many years during your working career did you get a $24,000 pay increase? If you've had a few, then you know the good feeling. If you never had a bump like that, then buckle your seatbelt: That's the kind of bump you can do every year, on just one property!

I'll let your imagination take it from here.

At a 10 cap rate, you've increased the value of your property by $240,000. And when measured by the extra buying power when you move that money into another deal with 20 percent down:

$240,000 value increase divided by .2 = $1,200,000 more property you can own! All due to a nuisance increase.

My friend, this is how you make *real money*.

WHEN IT MAKES SENSE TO CLEAN HOUSE

There are times when you won't want to keep *any* of the existing tenants and it's cause for celebration when they leave. This occurs when your property has been sliding down for a long time, and is brimming with undesirables. It also happens when you raise a property to a much higher class than it is now. For instance, if you raise a C– property to a B–, very few tenants can afford the higher rent you should be charging.

I've done this a few times. Early in my career, I bought a six-family property in a C section of the city—with real D tenants.

How could I tell they were D tenants? First, there were roaches everywhere in the building.

I mean everywhere. This property educated me on how to enter a dirty apartment. What you do is push the door open between rooms and stand back for a moment before you enter. Why? To let the roaches fall that hang out on top of the door. Yes, the roaches educated me that day.

(You find this happening only in D apartments. If you're not interested in D apartments—which you should not be for a while—don't worry about this little lesson. But it's entertaining if you didn't have to live through it, so read on.)

This six-family had roaches crawling all over the place in broad daylight. That's when you *really* have a problem: The roaches didn't try to hide, but walked around like they owned the place, because they did!

Along with the roaches, even lower forms of life inhabited the dump: a heroin dealer, crack dealer, and two pot dealers. Oh, and the rest of the tenants hadn't paid rent for a long while.

What in the world was I doing buying this property? Because I got it for one fantastic price, and it was in a decent area. I just had to find a way to get the drug dealers out and the property would be a winner.

I bought the property for $58,000. Before I closed, I worked out an arrangement with the local and state police departments to stake out the property. I agreed to give them access to the property whenever they wanted. In return, they would help get rid of the drug dealers.

The plan worked very well. Some snitch tipped off the dealers and within 30 days they scurried from that building like rats leaving a sinking ship.

Here's the thing with drug dealers: They usually have a thriving business that makes them lots of money. The last thing they want to do is get busted and go to the can. If you leave them alone, they will pay your rent on time and pay it in cash! But as soon as they think they've been discovered, they pack up shop and move on. They want to stay in business.

This little property has given me over $1,700 a month in positive cash flow over the years. It is now worth over $400,000. What a great performer.

On a larger-scale project, we recently bought a C– property with C– and D tenants in North Dallas. This area is being revitalized. The city and developers are tearing down a lot of C properties and building A properties and A retail establishments.

I'm shooting to take this 365-unit property from a C– to a C+ or even B–. The process is what you just read earlier: Do the exterior and common area repairs, and get rid of the slow-payers, non-payers, and criminals.

I'll have the interior of all units upgraded from their current condition to a grade higher. This includes all new paint, carpet, appliances, cabinet faces, counters, and lighting.

It will be done in phases. As we turn over the old tenants, we'll bring in the new. A transition of this size will take 24 to 36 months to complete. The purchase price was $9.5 million and we'll put

$2 million into the deal. Upon resale, we should realize a price of around $14.6 million.

I know you won't be doing a deal of that size this month. But you should soak up the concepts, which apply to both the 6-unit and the 365-unit deals.

When you get good at seeing beneath the surface, you can separate the gold mines from the land mines. Then, before you buy the property, your analysis will either confirm your suspicions, or you'll move on.

By the time you actually buy the property, your plan for realizing a substantial profit will already be in place. Then it's a matter of your team putting that plan into action.

IN THE NEXT CHAPTER

I hate numbers.

Let me be more specific: I love numbers when they're large ones attached to my bank account. However, I hate to *run numbers*, or analyze properties by crunching through a bunch of calculations. That's why I've reduced that necessary process to the fewest numbers possible.

Let's go through them in the next chapter, step by step. I think you will see they're all straightforward and not at all difficult to calculate.

CHAPTER 7

How to Analyze a Property Using the Fewest Numbers for the Most Profit

Now that you have your marketing game going, a lot of properties will be coming to you in a short period. You must have a quick and efficient way to determine whether you should take the next step and make an offer on a property.

When you create relationships with brokers, the first thing they'll do is put you on their e-mail list.

It's important that you respond to brokers within 24 hours, so that you can establish your professionalism with them. You may feel special because you're seeing these deals, but in reality you're only one name on a larger list that's receiving the e-mail at the same time you are.

As I mentioned in a previous chapter, you've become special only when brokers call you *before* deals hit the list. Until you get to that point, you must be hyper-responsive.

Most deals that get sent out this way are just average. A few brokerage companies, though, do business this way regardless of the listing. They e-mail their list, set a date for offers, and hope to create a bidding war.

When it's open bidding for a property, usually one or two buyers will offer a very high price for the property—a price that doesn't make sense based on the numbers. For some unknown reason, they make the crazy offer and of course win.

Very rarely do I win such an open offering. I usually don't even get involved, but when I do, I'm usually in the top five. Remember my three rules of doing business? Well, sometimes brokers will come to me after the original buyer falls through. Now they need a buyer with a proven track record, who does what he says he's going to do, makes doing business with him easy, and is not a pain in the butt. Your reputation is like money in the bank.

The seller went with the original highest offer because he couldn't control his greed glands. He fantasized about his huge profit, and didn't judge whether the buyer could actually close such a high offer. As it turns out, the buyer often cannot.

By being very responsive to brokers, you will start working your way up their preferred buyers list.

Here's a tip: Very few investors respond by phone to those e-mails. A few respond by e-mail, but the vast majority don't respond at all. You are going to stand out from the crowd because you'll call these brokers. You'll thank them for sending you the deal, even though you know you're just on the mass mailing list. Then you'll explain why the deal does or does not work.

Because they're usually not great deals, let's assume that this is the case.

Explain why it doesn't work, and then explain how you do like to buy (unit size, cap rate, and so on). Then ask: *Do you have any deals that fit those criteria?* Depending on how far up you are on his list, how much rapport you've built, you might get an: *Actually, I do have this one deal on the south side of town. . . .*

Then again, it may take more cultivating. At least you've started to train your brokers that you are a professional investor, this is how you buy, and you're different from other investors. Keep doing this, and sooner or later, those inner doors to the best deals will begin to swing open for you!

Back to the Cap Rate

Earlier in this book, I showed you how to determine a capitalization rate, or *cap rate*. In the commercial real estate world, the value of a property is determined by its cash flow and cap rate.

Let's discuss an important rule of thumb relating to cap rates. As you know, the cap rate equation is:

$$\text{Cap Rate} = \frac{\text{Net Operating Income (NOI)}}{\text{Value}}$$

To determine the value of the property, we just switch around the formula like this:

$$\text{Value} = \frac{\text{NOI}}{\text{Cap Rate}}$$

The type of property you are buying (A, B, C, or D) will determine what cap rate you use.

A simple definition of cap rate is the rate of return you expect to get on your investment. If you were buying a property that was newer and in a good area, this would be a less risky property to own, so you would expect to get a lower return.

If you're interested in a property in a tough area and it had a lot of deferred maintenance, you should expect to get a higher return.

Properties are categorized with letter grades. A's are good and D's are tough. Here's a refresher on each property type:

A properties were usually built within the last 10 years. Many white-collar workers live here. They are either renters by choice, or this is their last stop before buying a house. Your biggest competition in A properties is the single-family home market.

B properties were built within the last 20 years. Tenants are a mix of white-collar and blue-collar workers. This is where you'll start to see a little deferred maintenance on the property if it has not been taken care of properly.

C properties were built within the last 30 years. Units are filled mostly with blue-collar workers and tenants with Section 8 (subsidized housing) or other housing assistance. Contrary to popular belief, subsidized housing tenants can be a great population for your rental units. I rent to them all the time.

Sure, you need to screen those tenants more rigorously, and it does take more applicants to get the tenant you want. For instance, one of my criteria for Section 8 tenants is that they have a job. This shows me they are responsible. Having a job also means they will make their part of the rent payment, and the government will pay the rest.

Most of these people will never buy a house and will rent your units for life. If you treat them like the gold they are, they'll stay with you and provide you with cash flow for many years to come.

D properties were built more than 30 years ago. They are usually in bad areas, filled with very bad tenants. You may find a D property in a C or B area; if this is the case, you can probably reposition that property to a C or a B.

If the D property is in a lousy area, avoid it. I've invested in D properties and yes, you can make money from them. But it is *not fun*. Besides, you can make just as much money buying better quality properties in better areas.

The rule of thumb for cap rates for each of these property types is as follows:

A: 6–7

B: 8–9

C: 10–11

D: 12+

These are only rules of thumb. A hot market will move these cap rates down, because when demand is up, people are willing to accept lower returns. As the cap rate lowers, the property becomes more expensive.

Now that we have that established, let's go back to the properties brokers are sending you.

ANALYZING YOUR FIRST DEAL

Jack, one of the brokers you're cultivating, sends you a property. It's a 75-unit building. He gives you projected income and expense numbers and wants you to tell him if you like it. Now your task is to determine its value, and compare that to what the seller is asking for the deal.

Jack told you the income is $772,000 a year and expenses run $370,000 a year.

At this point you must engage another important rule of thumb to determine value. It deals with expenses.

Expenses on a 2-unit to 20-unit property will run about 35 to 40 percent of income. Expenses on larger properties will run about

50 percent of income. These numbers assume that tenants are paying the utilities.

Simply do a quick scan of the expenses: Are they at least 50 percent of the income?

$$\frac{\$370{,}000 \text{ in Expenses}}{\$772{,}000 \text{ in Income}} = 48\% \text{ Expense Ratio}$$

This one's a little low at 48 percent. If you want to be a conservative investor, then assume expenses will be a little higher, as in 50 percent.

You'll often see the expense figure come in much lower than the rule of thumb. When this happens, do *not* just assume it's a great deal and go with the lower numbers. Instead, *increase the figure to 50 percent and then do your calculations.*

Why? Because when the figures come in lower than the rule of thumb, it means one of three things—all of them bad:

1. The seller is not doing regular repairs.
2. The seller doesn't know the true expenses.
3. The seller is lying.

It's usually explanation number one, that the seller has been deferring the repair and maintenance.

If you're going to be successful at repositioning such a property, you'll have to spend more to make those repairs the first year and catch up.

It may not be one major repair, but a lot of little ones. Still, they can really add up and deplete your cash flow.

It could be that the seller is a lousy recordkeeper, and actually does not know the true expense picture. Believe it or not, many investors don't even know whether they're making a profit. They think they're doing okay because the cash flow arrives every month, but they're not accurately monitoring where that cash goes.

Then there are the liars. They know the property value is determined by the income and expenses. If they can show lower expenses, some of these desperate owners will do it.

The seller may even be adamant that the property is running at the lower expense level. In this situation, ask for copies of all previous invoices. If he says he doesn't have them, ask for permission to contact the vendors to get copies of invoices for the last two years.

You could even ask to see last year's bank reconciliation to verify who was paid and when. The bottom line is you *know* the property can't be run that cheaply. Do your numbers based on the higher expenses, and make any offers based on those more conservative numbers.

How Do We Know It Really Is a Deal?

You did the quick analysis and determined that the property looks good. The next step is to verify the numbers on both the income and expense side.

Verify income by requesting the last two years of profit-and-loss statements, the year-to-date profit-and loss-statement, and the current *rent roll.* That's a list of which tenants live in which units and how much they are paying in rent.

Compare the income shown on the current rent roll with the current month's income as stated by the seller. If they match up, great. If they don't, pretend you're Ricky Ricardo (Lucy's husband), and go back to the seller and tell him, *"You have a lot of splainin' to do."*

Here's an important principle: Act dumb.

Don't go barging in on the broker or the seller, acting like a know-it-all. Don't say: *Your numbers don't make sense.* If you do that, you've just made them defensive before they even know what you're talking about.

Instead, put the focus on you, by saying: *I must be missing something, because I can't seem to reconcile the income statement with the rent roll.* The beauty of that approach is you win either way: If you did miss something, you don't have egg on your face from a false accusation. If you didn't miss anything, they soon realize that you know more than you're letting on.

Two Years Tell the Tale

The last two years of profit-and-loss statements will tell you the financial story of a property.

This story will emerge from the *net income numbers* (that is, revenue minus expenses). When you get the last two years of profit-and-loss statements, it will most likely arrive in the form of a *trend report*. In other words, it will show the last 24 months of profit and loss, all nicely laid out in front of you.

Simply look at the total income line and see what it's been doing for the last 24 months. Has it been stable? Was it a steady riser? Did it experience a period of instability?

Do the same with the total expense line. You'll soon get a good idea of the history of the property.

I like to get these numbers *before* I make an offer. That way I really know what I'm dealing with. Unfortunately, they are not always available, and the seller or broker may only provide a *pro forma* profit-and-loss statement. In other words, a projected statement. They're saying that, based on the numbers they *project*, the property is worth X.

In other words, a projected statement. They're saying that, based on the numbers they *project*, the property is worth X.

I don't blame them for taking the easy route, but we want to base our offer on *actual results*. This is the way you create gold mines, which I talk about in Chapter 6.

CURRENT MANAGEMENT: WHEN TO HOLD 'EM AND WHEN TO FOLD 'EM

When you're buying smaller, 3-unit to 10-unit properties, there's a good chance the current management company is none other than the current owner. (Remember how most owners become landlords, who then become burned-out basket cases?) The way you evaluate their performance is by the numbers they give you.

If this is the case, you know you won't fall into the trap they did—being in the tenant business. You get a good qualified management company to run the property for you. I talk about how to do that in Chapter 11.

If there is outside management in place, you'll have to decide whether to keep them managing the property or to get rid of them. The way you decide is—again—by looking at the numbers.

Have they been collecting all the rents that are due, and have they kept occupancy high? Those are the top responsibilities of a manager. If either answer is *no*, then dump 'em.

You'll often hear this excuse: *Our hands were tied by the owner. He wouldn't pay for advertising or repairs.*

This is a common objection and in some cases it's even true. Still, a good management company will not stay at a property where the owner will not support the operations.

It quickly becomes a miserable place to work. Tenants call with repair requests, and soon become angry that they're not being done. Guess who is the target of that anger?

Morale in the office suffers and before you know it, that property is a very negative place to work. Good management companies are outta there, to be replaced by management that just doesn't care.

If the property is not running properly, get rid of the bad apples, but do keep an eye out for good employees in a bad situation.

When you take over the property, interview each employee and decide who stays and who goes. Yes, this is the job of the management company; but while you're doing your due diligence on the property, you should have a say in who will be the staff. It *will be* your property, after all.

Sometimes you'll find one or two gems in that mess. They do have pride in their work and were probably hanging on, hoping for something to change, and that change is you.

It's also good if you can keep one or two employees, because they know so much about the property. They're intimately aware of who are good and bad tenants, who's a good vendor, and who's a deadbeat. This will save you a lot of time and money to re-create.

The main reason you should get rid of most staff on a suffering property is because once bad habits are formed, they are very hard to break. It's much easier on both you and the tenants if you start fresh.

What If the Property Is Running Okay?

Getting rid of management that's doing a decent job is a tougher question. Once again, property records will give you the answer.

Ask to see copies of work orders. How long did it take to complete them? The answer should be between 24 and 48 hours.

Ask how long it takes to turn a vacant unit around and get it ready for the next tenant (that is, a *make ready*). The answer should be three days or less.

Look at the maintenance log. If there isn't one, this is not a good sign.

Check out the collections history file. They should be collecting 90 percent of rents due by the 15th of the month, and closing their books by the end of the month with only 1 to 3 percent of the rent outstanding. If they aren't doing this, they are not properly training their tenants. This directly affects your cash flow.

Ask what is the average tenant turnover. It should be around 40 percent or less of the property every year. The higher it is above that figure, the more tenant retention programs you'll need.

Walk the property. See whether the hallway walls are clean. Cobwebs, trash, and abandoned couches or mattresses are all negative signs.

This Simple Question Speaks Volumes

One of my favorite questions is: *What is your tenant retention policy?* What I'm really asking is: *What are you doing to keep the current tenants happy and staying in the property?*

This is a critical question, because the biggest expense you will incur on a regular basis is tenant turnover. It's important to minimize turnover as much as possible.

If they rattle off a 15-minute speech about everything they do to keep tenants happy—and if they all revolve around creating a *community*—then you may have a winning management company.

The more likely response: *Uh, we're very tenant focused, and um, we respond as quickly as we can when a tenant reports a problem.* Let me translate that response for you: Go find another management company.

It doesn't matter how big or how small the property is: As corny as it sounds, tenants want to know that you care about them. They also want to feel like they're part of some community.

It's easy to create these feelings, but that doesn't mean most management companies do it. All you need to do is a combination of simple acts like:

- Return phone calls promptly.
- Do repairs quickly.
- Have a party every so often.

- Send out a community newsletter (nothing more than a flyer).
- Arrange for discounts from local vendors.
- Hold a raffle.
- Have a contest for the best holiday display.

After you interview the management company, there's one more test: The gut check. After talking with the company and its employees, if a little voice makes you concerned about any of them, listen to that voice. It will be right 99 percent of the time.

WHAT MATTERS THE VERY MOST TO TENANTS

Of the hundreds of things you could do, the very most important is to be prompt in *returning their phone calls and dealing with their concerns.*

It sounds simple, and it is! But ignore these incredibly basic rules, and watch what happens:

- Tenants feel disrespected.
- Disrespected tenants complain to anyone who will listen, and poison the atmosphere.
- People leave as soon as they have the chance.

When repair requests come in, let tenants know that it will be done within 72 hours, unless it's an emergency. In that case, you'll get it done immediately.

Let them know when you will be there, so they don't have to guess. They will really appreciate this. Then make sure the repair is done *correctly*. There is nothing more frustrating than a repair that is not done right and the tenant must go through the whole repair request process a second time.

Make Small Investments for Big Returns

Show your appreciation to tenants by having your management company host regular get-togethers. Have a cookout in the summer, on Labor Day, and on other nice-weather occasions. Have holiday get-togethers and make them festive with inexpensive decorations. You will quickly create a community and your tenants will love it.

Have your management company solicit other vendors or businesses in the area for special discounts for your residents only. You can have a *business of the month*, so when they go to that business and mention your property, they get 10 percent or 20 percent off. It's just another win-win, with tenants loving it and businesses getting more traffic.

Community newsletters are a great way to keep the tenant base informed of what's going on and a great way to stay in touch with them every month. You can quickly fill a couple of pages when you:

- Explain any upgrades you're making to the property.
- Include a how-to section.
- Throw a favorite recipe in there.
- Describe a little program where if they pay their rent before the first of the month, they're entered in a raffle to win $50 or $100 (great for your cash flow).
- Announce when the next cookout will be, and so on.

You can use your computer's word processing program or many other software programs to create a simple newsletter. They are easy to create. Just get on the mailing list of many newsletters—whether they're on the Web or just in your town—and you'll soon have ideas for months in advance.

What if you have just a three-unit property? Send them a newsletter anyway! They'll appreciate it even more, because they know you're not sending it to hundreds of tenants. And they'll stay longer, too.

Holiday display contests are great. You can do this on Christmas, Easter, Halloween, or any other holiday. Whoever decorates an entryway the best wins a $50 prize. Have the tenants vote by secret ballot on the best one and watch the excitement. It not only gets everyone involved, but it makes your property look great during the holidays.

These aren't *expenses*; they're *investments*. Your payback will be tenants who stay longer, complain less, and keep your vacant units filled by telling their friends. Tenants will also absorb rent increases with less complaining.

IS SOMEONE PUTTING LIPSTICK ON A PIG?

When analyzing a property, just as important as the financials is the physical condition.

You need to walk the *entire* property, with your radar on full power. Look for any sign of problems.

Check out the trim and woodwork on the exterior. Is all the paint intact, and the wood smooth? If you see a lot of odd texture under the paint, the owner probably painted over rotted wood. It's so common that there's a term for it: *Lipstick*.

If there is a board on the very bottom of the siding, and it runs along the bottom all the way around, it's a red flag. This usually means the wood beneath is rotted and they didn't want to replace the siding.

Take a look at the windows: Are they in good working order?

Check out any brick: Are there any long, vertical cracks? This is a settling problem, and it may or may not be major.

Are the corners of the shingles starting to rise on the roof? This is a sign of age. The roof is a major expense, not only for labor and materials, but also because you may lose rental income while some units are open to the blue sky.

You must factor in any roof repair at the time of purchase. If you cross your fingers and hope you can just flip this property quickly to another buyer who can worry about the roof, you'll be sorry. Sure, hold off on repairs for as long as you can, but negotiate right up front to get a price break to pay for that roof while you own the property.

Is the grass greener in certain areas? This usually means one of two things: You've just found the location of the septic system, or a pipe is broken underground.

If it's the latter, either the seller's or your contractor must dig up those pipes and fix them. This has happened to me, and it can be costly. Ask tenants if they've seen people fixing pipes. If they tell you that pipes break all the time, this is a big problem.

If you're considering a property with buildings built on slab foundations, you may run into a common problem. In some parts of the country, copper pipes react with the local cement mixture. Over time the pipes deteriorate and start to leak in the slabs.

This is a very costly repair. You will usually see very high water bills on a property when it has this problem. Ask your inspector to take special care to investigate that particular problem.

Also look for standing water. It's a sign of a high water table or broken pipes.

When walking the property, walk the perimeter. Check out who your neighbors are. Are they all residences for a couple of blocks away, or are there businesses within sight?

If there are businesses, what kind are they? There's a greater chance of toxic substances being released onto your property if there are gas stations, dry cleaners, or storage facilities nearby.

Why *storage facilities?* Because people store toxic chemicals in barrels and never come back. Those barrels deteriorate and toxic substances leak into the ground, near your property. Be very afraid.

If you see any empty lots, call the city and ask whether any permits have been *pulled*, or applied for. If so, who pulled them and what are they building? If not, go to the registry of deeds and see who the owner is and when the property changed hands.

Did someone just pull a permit for adult dancing, or a day care center? The answer will make a big difference in your life if you own the property next door.

Take a look at any pool on the property. Is the water clean? If not, this could be an indication of problems with the pump or filter system. Also see whether the patio concrete is intact.

If you get rid of a pool by filling it in, because it's an eyesore, that can help to reduce your costs. Just don't try this on an A or B property, where the pool is a major amenity. If it's a C property, then the decision depends on what your competition is doing: If they have a pool, then don't fill in yours. If they filled theirs in or never had one, you might consider filling yours in.

LET'S LOOK INSIDE

It's now time for the interior inspection. It's not the same inspection that your property inspectors will do, though. They'll look at all the structural components that need trained professionals to evaluate. They'll also *survey* the apartment units, meaning they will go into a sample of them. If they like what they see, they stop. If they discover problems, they'll go into more.

You will go into *all of the units*. You can't do this until you have the property under agreement, so this step is after you've done your financial and exterior analysis.

I know it can be boring to go into dozens or even hundreds of units. But why do you suppose that I will still take a day or even several days out of my schedule to walk a property, even though I control more than $140 million of property?

Because you must never *assume* when it comes to your investment. The units you decide to skip to save a little time might be the ones that reveal a major roof leak, black mold, or some other profit-busting problem. And you know what they say in the military: *Don't assume—or it will make an ASS out of U and ME.*

When going into the units, keep your eyes open for anything not right: carpet, walls, kitchen counters, cabinets, faucets, appliances, water stains in ceilings, bathroom fixtures, doors, and so on. As I mentioned before, what you're really looking for is a *problem common throughout the complex.*

Some common problems are older items that will need replacing during your ownership. You need to come up with an estimate of those costs. If the problems will cost more money than you anticipated—or than what the seller estimated—it's time to consider renegotiating the price or getting a repair allowance at the closing.

MARKET AREA INSPECTION

We've looked at the numbers, the exterior, and the interior of the property. Now it's time to consider the market area and make sure we are in the right place at the right time.

If you read my first book, *Emerging Real Estate Markets*, you know the four phases of the market cycle and the correct strategy to use in each phase.

The overall objective is to invest in markets that are still considered soft, but certain key indicators suggest they are about to take off.

Occupancy

The first key indicator is occupancy. What is the overall occupancy in the city right now? You must know this because it should calibrate the expectations for your property, and whether you can make money at that occupancy.

Find this number by asking management companies or commercial real estate brokers in the area.

But Dave, I plan to invest in small three-unit to six-unit properties; how can this relate to me?

It relates to you all right, because the overall occupancy indicates the health of that market. You also should find out average occupancy for the last 24 months, so you can gauge trends.

If it's been going from 88 to 94 percent over those months, you're in a healthy market. You have a good chance to raise rents. If your market has been doing the opposite, it will be more challenging. Though you may not be able to raise rents, you still can make money as long *as you did your buying analysis based on this market condition.*

Do not buy a property based on a rosy forecast! In fact, you might even want to drop projected income by 10 percent in your analysis, because that might be where you're headed.

You can make money in both types of situations, though the strategies differ. In a down market, buy for cash flow. Your property is not appreciating, so you have to get your return from operations. In an up market, buy for appreciation.

The Jobs Profile

What are jobs doing in the area? Occupancy trends will give you a pretty good indication of the job market: If jobs are coming into an area, occupancy naturally goes up. Job growth is an absolutely vital indicator in any market.

Here's one of the best situations you can ever hope for: Jobs are coming into an area, yet there is a limited supply of apartments. Demand quickly outstrips supply, and apartment owners benefit from both cash flow and appreciation.

In such markets, occupancy reaches 95 percent and higher. At 95 percent occupancy, you should start to raise rents.

Sometimes you'll even find a market that keeps ahead of supply growth. This means jobs continue to stream in, and builders can't build enough apartments to meet that demand.

If you're already in that market, this is very good news. Just be on your toes, because eventually those builders *will* catch up—and the dumb ones will keep on building more units!

Then the market will become oversupplied. There will be many more units available than are needed and rents will level off. As builders continue building, you may have to give incentives to get people to move in to your building.

The incentives might be one-half month of free rent; no security deposit; a $99 first-month special—there are dozens of marketing techniques you can use.

If you want many more ideas, just go to www.MultiFamilyMillions.com and type in the keyword *management*.

THE SIDEWALK TELLS THE STORY

When buying a property that you think is a B property, please make sure it's in a B area! If you buy a B property in a C area, it will become a C very soon.

Buying a B property in an A area can sometimes work out: Your rents will probably be at the high end of the spectrum, and your B property will be worth more than B's in the B area.

Naturally, you can do the same by buying a C property in a B area. By doing so, you're *repositioning upward.*

One of the easiest ways to tell what kind of area you are in is to look at the retail businesses. Are they high-end (nice restaurants), middle-of-the-road (an office supply store) or low-end (pawn shops)? Whatever retail is in the area, this is the type of tenant your building will attract.

It's also important to note the *trend* in local retail. Have major chains moved out or in? Is middle class retail being replaced by lower-end or higher-end stuff? Knowing this will give you an excellent indication of where this market is going and whom you can attract to your building.

When looking at retail, also pay attention to culture and ethnicity. What *kinds* of restaurants are in the area? What types of clothing stores are common? This tells you who shops there and what your tenant profile should be.

Investors often make the mistake of renovating for a target profile that's not substantially present in the three-mile community around them. Don't try to change demographic trends by yourself! Ride this powerful wave instead, and profit from it.

BUT WHAT IF MY NUMBERS ARE OFF?

You may discover that—based on all the many factors we've just talked about—your numbers are off. If they're *way off*, it's time to renegotiate.

This business is about marketing, but it's also about numbers. You must buy a property based only on:

- Your buying criteria of how much cash flow and profit you want to make; and
- Your findings into how that property has historically done, what repairs are necessary, and the trends you've uncovered in that area.

If the original numbers don't work for you now, renegotiate until they do. Do *not* rationalize the deal, convincing yourself that you *can* make the numbers work after you buy. That is a fool's game, and you'll soon be broke if you go there.

Also, do not become emotionally attached to any deal. This is why your marketing system is so critical: If you know there are plenty of deals where this one came from, you'll be able to walk away, if necessary. Your chance of negotiating will also be better, because the seller—just like horses—will sense if you're a confident person or not.

DON'T GET DEPRESSED ON ME!

I know you may be thinking: *Whoa, Dave! This property analysis stuff sounds like work! I'm not up to it.*

Remember three things:

1. You do your initial analysis from the comfort of your home or office; only when you have a *live one* on your hands will you ever bother to go look at it.
2. You're not doing this work all by yourself. I talk in Chapter 14 about how you can have a team of people do much of the work for you, and how you're not necessarily paying them out of your pocket.
3. Keep your eye on the payday! You don't need many of these deals to be set for a year, a decade, or even for *life!*

IN THE NEXT CHAPTER

Don't be *all dressed up with no place to go.* I don't want you to know every method for finding great deals, only to be stopped dead in your tracks because you can't finance them.

The fantastic thing about real estate is that it's not a vicious cycle: You do *not* need to have money to make money. I explain why in the next chapter.

CHAPTER 8

WHERE TO GET THE MONEY FOR ALL YOUR DEALS

You've been fed a pack of lies.

When you listen to the late-night TV gurus, you hear that real estate investing is possible with *no money down*. In one sense that's true, because many deals can be structured so you personally don't put any cash down. (I'll show you how to get that money from partners.) But that's different from believing that the only good real estate deals are ones where no one is making a down payment.

Sure, a few deals can work that way. But why limit yourself? If you can get an excellent deal that requires 20 percent down—but you don't have to use your own money—why not do it?

Stated another way: You shouldn't be looking for *no-money-down* deals; you should be looking for *no-money-out-of-YOUR-pocket* deals.

In this chapter, I explain how to get money from lenders who will give you 80 to 90 percent of the money you need. Then I tell you where to get the rest of the money.

Just so you know, you'll always be needing money! When you're starting out broke, you need it for obvious reasons. Then, when you make a pile of money, you can temporarily finance your own deals.

I say *temporary*, because one day you're taking a shower and come to realize what an idiot you've been: You're quite successful and now finance all your own deals. But it dawns on you that you could have done 100 to 300 percent more deals if you were financing them with other people's money.

Even Donald Trump laments that he'd much rather hang out at home with his shoes off. Instead, he is out on the town most nights, schmoozing with more potential financing sources for his next giant venture.

So let's demystify the world of financing your deals.

WHY BANKS LIKE APARTMENTS

I know this comes as a big surprise to you, but banks are conservative. They want to get their loans back. They've been burned when markets suddenly get very soft, and suddenly thousands of loans in the same area become jeopardized.

These conservative bankers will be happy to discover that over the next several years, we will see a positive phenomenon that has not happened in this country since the 1960s.

Back then, *Baby Boomers* came of age. They left their parents' homes and moved into apartments. That Boomer wave for the rental market lasted a decade. Investors who owned apartments routinely became millionaires. There was more demand than supply and developers worked overtime to keep up.

Forget all the fine points about apartment investing: In those days, as long as you ran your apartments semi-competently, you couldn't go wrong. That rising tide lifted all boats.

We're now seeing the same phenomenon, though it's not due to Baby Boomers. It's their kids, the *Echo Boomers*, who will be causing all the ruckus.

For the next 8 to 15 years, Echo Boomers entering the apartment market will create demand not seen since their parents started renting.

To make matters better for apartment owners, the immigrant population is surging. These two demographic forces are like an unstoppable *tsunami* that will wash over smart apartment owners with a monstrous wave of money.

I say *smart* apartment owners, because the dummies are gonna get slaughtered. They will wait to invest in apartments until the wave has been going full-bore for years, after most real fortunes have been made. They'll want to feel comfy, investing after that long run-up in prices.

The smart investors will instead see the great demographic movements just a little sooner. Well-trained pilots trust their instruments and can reach their destination in almost any weather. Amateurs in both aviation and investing like to operate by the seat of their pants.

Back to lenders: Your friendly neighborhood home loan officer may or may not see this trend coming, but commercial lenders who lend on apartments are becoming aware of it. That's why so many of them like apartments.

THREE FLAVORS OF LENDERS

Three types of traditional companies will finance your deals: *local*, *national*, and *conduit* lenders.

Local lenders are the savings and loan institutions in your hometown. They're also the banks that do the commercial loans. Their strengths are:

- They like to deal with local people.
- They know the market.
- They know the players and the properties.
- They can get things done very quickly.

If you're investing in your own backyard, definitely establish relationships with local lenders. One easy way to start is open an account. If you then tell them you'll also open an operating account for the property you're buying, well, that's sweet music!

You're their new best friend for two reasons: Accounts generate nice fees and interest spreads. That's the difference between what the account actually earns in interest, and what they pay you.

The second reason has to do with banking regulations. Bankers can only lend money based on a certain multiple of how much they have in deposits. And the more they can lend, the more they make in mortgage-lending revenue.

Sometimes, to get a loan, a bank will require you to open an account. Don't wait for them to ask! Do it right away, and you'll make it easier to do the deal.

Once you establish a relationship with local lenders, you can get things done very quickly. They'll even help you out of a jam when you need it.

For example, I purchased a 396-unit property that needed repositioning. I went with a national lender with whom I had done business recently. Everything went well—until three weeks before the closing, when the lender decided it didn't want to do the deal!

I was in shock. The numbers were very solid on that deal. At the last minute, they simply decided they didn't want to get involved in a repositioning of that size.

I was in jeopardy of losing $130,000 in deposits if I didn't close on time. It was a $6,000,000 loan. I turned to a local lender who had financed another deal for me in the past. They picked up the ball and were able to close the deal in the time I needed.

Typically, this closing should have taken a minimum of 45 days for the local lender, but we worked together and they got it done.

Here's the flip side: When you are coming from out of state, local lenders there will initially be cautious. Some will simply not do business with you if you don't live in the state.

So get down there and spend some face time with them, in the form of lunch. Afterward, stay in contact with them regularly. This technique is what allowed me to do my first deal in that market with a local lender, and why that lender helped me out of the jam I was in.

One downside with local lenders is their rates tend to be higher than with national lenders. This affects your cash flow and profitability.

They also like to amortize loans for shorter periods: 15 to 20 years, versus national lenders that will go 25 to 30 years. This means you'll have to pay down principal faster. Sometimes these higher monthly payments make it more difficult to get the numbers to work.

This is okay if you plan on holding the property for the long term. But when you're buying for relatively quick cash flow and appreciation, this works against you.

The primary reason to use local lenders outside of your area will be for repositioning deals. Local lenders will give you the best construction and bridge loans.

Roughly speaking, they'll lend at 70 to 80 percent of the value so you can purchase the property; then they'll give you another 70 to

80 percent of the construction cost to reposition the property. This will cost 1 to 2 points (that is, 1 to 2 percent of the loan amount), and the interest rate will also be a point or two higher than the conventional rate.

You can often get a *rollover provision,* which allows the loan to roll over to a predetermined fixed rate once your property is stabilized. That's good because you won't incur any additional costs for this end-loan financing. Of course, it's not so good if interest rates move on you too much, and the rolled-over rate is no longer competitive in the marketplace.

National Lenders

National lenders have no problem lending on properties all around the country. Most of these lenders sell their loans on the secondary market to Freddie Mac and Fannie Mae. That allows them to reduce their loans outstanding (remember, they can lend only in a fixed ratio to their deposits). With those loans off their books, they're free to go back out into the marketplace, write more loans, and make even more money.

Because these lenders sell loans to the secondary markets, they must conform to the standards set forth by Freddie Mac, Fannie Mae, or any other player they are selling their loans to.

They call these loans *the package:* The loans must be properly packaged so they can be sold. Here are some of the packaging requirements for properties:

- Occupancy has been 85 percent or better for at least the last three months, and in some cases, six months.
- Debt coverage ratio is 1.2 or better. This ratio is calculated by dividing net operating income by the mortgage debt service. Put another way, lenders want to see that for every dollar you have in debt service, you have $1.20 coming in to cover it. Some lenders require this number to be 1.25. In tight markets, almost all lenders increase the ratio to 1.25.
- Secondary markets don't like to take properties that need a lot of repairs. Sometimes they require that the cost of repairs be escrowed at closing until those repairs are made.

- They want to see stabilized profit-and-loss statements from the previous six months. They do not want erratic financials, because it's often a warning sign of a problem property.
- They also like to see income and expense numbers that are stable or at least getting better. If they judge the numbers to be too erratic, they'll require that you put more money down on the property.
- Freddie Mac and Fannie Mae typically don't like to fund properties with flat roofs because of their higher maintenance costs. They have done it, but not often.

CONDUITS

Conduit lenders are very much like national lenders but they usually get their money from major lenders on Wall Street. They then sell their loans to life and casualty companies, large investors, and pension funds. Whoever may be in the market to buy a package of loans, conduit lenders will sell a package to them.

Conduit lenders are more flexible than national ones. Their guidelines are not as strict and because of this, you may be able to fund more deals through them.

Their rates are a bit higher than from national lenders, but it's often a good tradeoff so you can get the deal done.

Some conduit lenders will be okay with seeing numbers from the last three months instead of six months. Most conduit lenders will finance flat roofs.

Each type of lender has its place. Yes, you must start somewhere, and it probably will be with a local lender. But you know from reading the earlier chapters that you're in the *cultivation* business: While you're cultivating brokers and other sources for deals, you should be cultivating as many lenders as you can.

WHEN TO USE A MORTGAGE BROKER

Whether you're just starting out or you're a veteran, mortgage brokers will be key players on your team.

Brokers have relationships with all major players in the mortgage banking industry. They know who does what, and whom to avoid for any given deal. A good mortgage broker will also prepare your loan to make it as saleable as possible to lenders.

They will cost around 1 percent of the loan, but will usually save you even more.

Had I used a mortgage broker on that deal I told you about, where the lender backed out, I would have been told that the lender is excellent in every area *except repositionings*. I learned that the hard way and it nearly cost me $130,000.

PUTTING YOUR PACKAGE TOGETHER

Let's say you've determined which type of lender is best for your next deal. The next step is to put the loan package together so you can submit it to the lender, also known as the *underwriter*.

Here's the principle you should follow: *Answer the question in the underwriter's mind before it is asked.*

That means you want to submit a *complete* package. Here are the components:

- Your resume.
- A description of the deal.
- Key dates, such as when the due diligence period expires, the expiration of the financing contingency, and the closing date for the property.
- Explain how you plan to operate the property (all the rental techniques we've covered in earlier chapters). Also give your summary on when and how the property will reach break-even, and then how you plan on paying back the lender.
- The last two years of financial statements of the property.
- A current year-to-date profit-and-loss statement.
- A current rent roll.

What a coincidence: You're giving the underwriter exactly what you requested to do your own financial due diligence. Why? Because the underwriter will want to do its own review, and needs that same information.

If this is your first deal, the underwriter will naturally focus on your ability to manage the property effectively, whether it's a three-family or a 300-unit deal.

Handle this objection right up front by including the resume of your management company, together with its marketing plan and a five-year profit-and-loss projection. You have just shown the underwriter that even though *you* may not have the experience to manage the property, you're a pro: You are smart enough to delegate that to a management company having many years of experience with just this type of property.

Be sure to include pictures of the property, plus an aerial map. You can get good aerial maps from googleearth.com.

Highlight the strengths of the project, and also *sell the sizzle:* Is the property on a main road? Make sure the lender knows that. Does it have a lot of green space? Is it especially solid construction in some respect?

Include whatever features and benefits you can possibly think of. Even though some may seem obvious, still bring them to the attention of the underwriter.

Be sure you include a signed purchase-and-sale agreement in the package. It must be signed by both parties. The lender will not start the process until it has a signed purchase and sale agreement, because without that document, there is no actual potential deal, just wishful thinking.

When you anticipate the underwriter's questions by providing all this material in advance, you come across like a real professional. Your deal will rise to the top of the deal pile on the underwriter's desk.

How to Get Partners to Fund Your Deals

All the lenders I've just described will require some level of down payment. Sometimes, that last 10 to 20 percent is the hardest to come by.

Fortunately, you can often turn to other people for those remaining dollars.

One excellent way to fund the remaining equity needed is to get it from your sellers. Owners will frequently finance from 10 percent of the deal, all the way up to the entire deal! There are a variety of reasons why sellers might agree to this; suffice it to say that you'd be surprised at how easy this type of financing is to get.

It is typical to get 10 to 20 percent seller financing. You do this by giving the seller a second mortgage on the property. Then you make your regular monthly payments on that note to the seller.

Sometimes you can arrange for the note to have no interest payments, but just a lump-sum due at the end. That one payment includes any calculated interest rate you agreed upon.

The note may also have a *balloon* tied to it. That means the second mortgage needs to be paid off on a predetermined date, and not steadily paid off (or *amortized*) over a long period.

There are countless variations and creative approaches to financing terms, so I don't want to get too deep into them here. Just keep this in mind: Cash flow is king in the multi-family game. It is the lifeblood of your investment. You want as much cash flow as you can get at any given time. This is why I like to let interest accumulate and pay it all off when the note comes due.

Be careful when getting a second mortgage from your seller. There are a lot of lenders that don't allow secondary financing. If that's the case, you'll have to skip the seller financing, even if the seller was ready and willing!

What are your alternatives if the lender doesn't allow second mortgages? Find a lender that does. Start dialing and ask. It may take many *no* answers to find that first *yes*, but it's worth it. At my *Unlimited Private Money* live event, I give out a list of 50 lenders and what they specialize in. My students know exactly whom to use for the deal they are structuring. For more information on that event, just go to MultiFamilyMillions.com and type in the keywords *private money*.

THE BIG, PROFITABLE WORLD OF PRIVATE MONEY

Second mortgages are great, but if you really want to explode your business, you'll need *private money* sources.

You should always be doing three things: marketing, getting private money, and expanding your knowledge. If you focus on these three things regularly, you will be unstoppable in real estate.

Once you have your private money system down, you'll be able to do as many deals as you wish, without using your own cash.

Private money refers to individuals, instead of the institutions we just talked about, lending you money.

All sorts of people have the potential to lend you money:

- Friends and family members
- People you work with, including your employer
- People in your social groups or your kids' sports groups
- Advisers like your attorney, accountant, or doctor
- In short, just about anyone with whom you have regular contact

Don't get the wrong idea here: I'm not talking about hitting up your friends, family, and others for cash. I do *not* mean: "Hey, can you lend me some money to do this deal?"

I call that begging. Instead, I'm talking about a business proposition where you are not dealing from a position of weakness, but of opportunity. You don't beg or cajole; you simply make the opportunity known and see whether the other party is interested. More on that later.

I once saw a study to the effect that 75 percent of all private money comes from friends and family members. A good portion of that money comes from their IRAs.

Yes, that's right—people can invest in your deals through their IRAs. I know: Your bank or brokerage firm never told you about that. In fact, if you went to a brokerage firm and specifically asked, "Can I hold real estate deals in my self-directed IRA?" they'd look at you like you're an idiot, and would say: "Of *course*, you can't."

They're the idiots. To be more specific, they're the greedy liars.

Here's the scam they're running: There are IRAs, and then there are self-directed IRAs. Banks and brokerage firms tell you they have a self-directed IRA, when in reality they've carefully designed the IRA to include only the investments that make them the most money.

They have truly directed the IRA to include only these investments, leaving you with the illusion that you're self-directing the investments from among those choices. You're being treated like a kindergartner in a sandbox. Mommy puts only the toys she wants you to play with in the sandbox, and you're completely free to play with them any way you choose.

Well, there's a whole breed of IRA for grownups that's available—the *true* self-directed IRA. Yes, there are government rules about what an IRA can and cannot hold, but those rules are much broader than most companies will tell you.

These IRAs are available from a bunch of companies throughout the United States. Why haven't you heard of them? Because they don't have $10 million to blow on a Super Bowl ad. And all they do is administer self-directed IRAs. They don't make a profit from whacking you for fees in all the investments you put into the IRA. They're honest operators that simply charge you for maintaining this IRA receptacle into which you put your investments, real estate, and so on.

And for the record, I don't have any financial relationships with these companies, so I'm not telling you this to make a buck off you. To get a list of some of these companies, just go to MultiFamilyMillions .com and type in the keyword *IRA*.

Here's why this IRA stuff is such a good opportunity for you: Most people earn lousy returns in their IRAs. A few of those people will jump at the chance to own local real estate in their IRAs, but never thought that was even an option.

You can offer that ability to invest in real estate, get monthly cash flow, and participate in the profits when the deal is resold. Of course, all the proceeds go right back into the IRA until they reach retirement age. But one or two deals pouring cash flow and appreciation into the account—and growing tax-deferred until retirement—really has the potential to explode that IRA balance.

Once you get the information from one or two companies (see my Internet list), you'll be able to explain to potential investors just how to switch their fee-grabbing IRAs over to truly liberated, truly self-directed ones.

You'll find a lot of people will thank you for opening their eyes to this brokerage-firm scam, and to the new possibilities with a superior IRA. In my case, of the tens of millions of dollars I've raised, approximately 42 percent of it has come from investors' IRAs.

As you're cultivating your contacts for potential investors, what you're really looking for are *angel investors*. They are high-net-worth people who like to invest in businesses and real estate.

Angel investors are easier to deal with because they've been through the investing process before. They know what to expect.

Angel investors usually invest from $50,000 to $5 million. In very general terms, they expect first-year cash returns to range from 7 to 10 percent or more; and they want to see annualized returns after the resale to be 20 to 25 percent and even higher. In exchange, they understand you'll need the use of their money for five to seven years.

Oh, and they expect you to get an acquisition fee. That's money you get up front for bringing the deal and the investors together. An average acquisition fee is between 1 and 5 percent of the deal. If you put together a $1 million deal, then a 3 percent fee would be $30,000. Imagine if you're doing a multimillion dollar deal!

Let me just hammer this into your brain: If you structure your deals along the lines of what I've just described, you not only put zero dollars of your own into the property, but you're *paid* to do the deal. That's why you must make it a top priority to cultivate your private money sources!

You may or may not be surprised to know that friends and family will give you the hardest time as private money investors. Every Thanksgiving they'll moan about your taking five to seven years for the deal to conclude (even though it may take as short as three to five years), and they'll nitpick at your acquisition fee.

They'll first ask you to explain the fee. Then you'll get the guilt-laden comment about just how much money it is, and if you think it's fair.

Oh, it's fair, all right. *You* are the one taking time out of your life to discover how to invest, then taking the time to create relationships, pursue lots of dead ends, and many other aspects to putting a deal together. You deserve that fee.

Always remember that you're not begging; you are offering an excellent opportunity. If some people start arguing with you about the fee or other such aspects, you need to have one single word in mind: *Next.* In other words, you need to move on to another person who will not drag you down with negativity and guilt, but will say: "Hey, that sounds interesting; tell me more."

When talking with angel investors, be ready to hand them your business plan. This will show that you are a professional and are prepared to see your vision through. You'll close more investors with a well-thought-out business plan. Your success with this investment opportunity will also be higher for the very fact that you've thought out that plan.

(If you've never written a business plan, go to www.bplan.com and get some ideas on how to do it.)

The other item to give investors is the property package. That document outlines the deal and gives all current and projected financials. It includes demographics of the city where the property resides and explains financing, closing costs, and all other major facts about the deal. This document allows investors to make well-informed decisions.

Be sure you do not sugarcoat the situation; include any negative aspects to the deal, too. This is a full-disclosure document. *Disclose everything*. Believe me: If you paint an unrealistically rosy picture now, then even an okay deal will turn out looking like a disappointment to investors who were expecting only spectacular results.

Always err on the side of being conservative and honest. You do not want investors coming after you later, claiming that you didn't tell them everything you knew. They may claim that the missing information would have affected whether they would have invested in the first place.

When you pool a group of investors together to buy a property, you are almost certainly creating a security. The Securities and Exchange Commission, together with regulators in all 50 states, have very detailed rules about how securities must be offered.

I know it costs money, but if you're going to raise money through securities, you must have on your team a good *securities attorney* who specializes in this area of the law.

During my *Unlimited Private Money* live event, I have an experienced attorney cover some of the laws relating to this area, which is known as *syndicating deals*.

DEBT VERSUS EQUITY DEALS

Your deal will either be structured as a debt partnership or an equity partnership. Debt partnerships are the cheapest way to fund your deals: You offer a certain interest rate as a return on their investment that is secured by real estate.

Let's say Joe and Mary Smith decide to invest $100,000 in your deal. You offered them a 10 percent return on their money. They would get 10 percent per year in simple interest on the money they invested.

I suggest you use simple interest and not compounded interest. If it compounds, you will pay them a lot more money over time.

This is the cheapest way to fund your deals because you get all the equity in a deal. You can sometimes go one step further and add a provision that states the interest will be paid only at the time of refinance or resale.

Doing this means you can avoid paying monthly interest. Remember that cash flow is king in our business. I would rather put off making payments until later so I can preserve my cash flow, even if I had to offer a slightly higher interest rate.

Equity partnerships are the other form of partnership you might form. This is the fastest way to fund your deals, because you're giving up part of that precious equity. Not only will your partners get monthly cash flow, but they'll share in any profits at the resale of the property.

Equity partners typically get between 50 and 75 percent of the deal. Does that sound high? Keep in mind that they're putting up the money for the deal (not to mention your acquisition fee). I discovered a long time ago that my getting a 25 or 50 percent share of something is a whole lot better than my keeping 100 percent of nothing.

One excellent way to find people to fund your deals is through the power of *association*. You want to associate with the right people; that is, people who have money. There are three stepping stones to them:

1. Church
2. Charitable organizations
3. Business organizations

Sometimes it's possible to forge excellent business relationships with people who share a common interest of yours. Whether you're both from the same church, or you both are part of some environmental group in your community, these are excellent rapport-builders.

You have something in common, which makes conversation easier. You can then find an appropriate time and place to mention your investment opportunities.

Will this be regarded as pushy? I don't think so. Consider this: If you were in the market to find a great plumber because you need work done in your house, would you be offended if a church acquaintance happened to mention that his friend was a great plumber? Hard-sells are a different story; but friends connecting with friends is a good thing.

Needless to say, you should be networking at the local chamber of commerce, Rotary Club, and other organizations where businesspeople are found. These groups almost always contain many, if not all, of the influential, richer members of the business community in your area.

Volunteer for different projects and to get onto boards of directors, even if it means doing laborious tasks at first. The people running those outfits once started at the bottom, too. They respect people who also volunteer.

There are many other ways to attract angel investors: You can hold a seminar or luncheon and target certain demographics. At my *Unlimited Private Money* live event, you'll watch me do the presentations and then you'll take home a DVD so you can practice them yourself. Some are as short as 30 seconds—just enough time to ride in an elevator with someone. Others are up to 30 minutes. You'll quickly become comfortable with all of them.

IN THE NEXT CHAPTER

I've negotiated more than 500 transactions as a real estate investor. I think I'm pretty good at it. In fact, I think I could probably get many other people to cave in and give me a better-than-fair deal.

But that would be *win-lose* negotiating, and I'm all about *win-win* deals. I want to forge long-term relationships, and those only come when people are satisfied with deals, and don't wake up one day realizing they've been had.

In the next chapter, you discover how to negotiate on a *win-win* basis. I also explain how you can not only stop *dreading* negotiations, but actually *look forward* to them!

CHAPTER 9

TWELVE NEGOTIATING SECRETS OF THE PROS

It's easy to fear negotiating when you've never really done it. All sorts of scenarios enter your head: *Will I be too easy and lose my shirt?. . . Will I be too tough and lose the deal?. . . What if I look unsure of myself?. . .* and so on.

I've found that knowledge and skill have a way of making shadowy fears disappear. Over a great many transactions, I've collected 12 favorite methods for negotiating confidently and with positive results. Though none of these methods was handed to me on an ancient scroll, you still might call them *secrets*, because so few people practice them.

1. BE PREPARED

Here's a great example of what I mean by *secrets*: If the advice to *be prepared* is so obvious, why don't more people follow it?

Again, *common sense* does not mean *common practice*. Given how few people do their homework before a negotiation, if you prepare, you'll already have scored an advantage!

I'm talking about discovering everything you can about the property, financials, and people behind the deal you're considering.

Do Your Homework on the Property . . .

Do you have any contacts in the area, like property managers or brokers? Have them drive by the property. What's the condition? What do they see that's out of the ordinary? Ask them about what they observe about the neighbors, what is the property near, and is there any standing water on the property. Do they know any stories about the property or neighborhood?

You can even call the police department and explain that you're thinking of buying a property, and does the officer you talk with have any opinion of the area? Depending on the person who answers the phone, you could get either a "We don't give out that type of information," or "Sure, we know that neighborhood well and it's fine/okay/terrible. . . ."

Then Do Your Homework on the Numbers . . .

You should have done your financial due diligence by getting profit-and-loss statements for the last two years, the year-to-date profit-and-loss numbers, and the current rent roll. In Chapter 7 I discussed how to make those numbers tell you the story about that property.

With most of the properties you'll be repositioning, the past story reads like a tragedy, and sometimes a comedy. But going over those numbers ahead of any negotiation will do two things:

1. It will make the seller know you're a professional who's maybe not worth trying to fool.
2. You won't miss any glaring problems with the financials that should be negotiated.

And Finally, Do Your Homework on the People

It used to be more difficult, but now the billionaires over at Google have made it surprisingly easy to get fairly detailed information on the parties you'll be facing in the negotiation. Google the following, and see what you come up with:

- Seller's name
- Seller's company name

- Property name
- City where the property is located

I was once negotiating on a 500-unit portfolio. I did my usual due diligence on the seller beforehand. I discovered the seller was from outside the United States, and owned seven other complexes in the United States. Three of those properties were in foreclosure or had already been taken back by the banks.

I also discovered that there was a federal court order for him to sell his other properties in the United States within a certain period or else he would go to prison. Do you think this information gave me just the slightest competitive advantage?

Don't stop at just Google. If you're dealing with a real estate broker, then ask that broker for as much information as possible about the seller: who he is, why he is selling, how many other assets he owns, when he needs to close by, what he plans to do with the money, and so on. You may not get much information, but then again, you may get a lot. You simply must ask to find out. It's what the pros do.

It Works Both Ways

Before entering a negotiation, expect the other party to Google *you*. Is there anything online that you'll need to explain? You must be prepared.

In fact, you should *consider* bringing any negative information up in the course of the conversation. It might not be necessary, but then again it might: For instance, you're interested in buying a property, yet there's a bankruptcy on your record from two years ago. The seller may need comforting that you have financing lined up. At the very least, have your answer prepared in case such topics come up.

2. Understand the Other Party's Needs

If you google a seller's name and discover he *needs* to sell properties quickly, you've just discovered a *primary need*. Another example might be that the seller is consolidating and moving out of the area. Knowing about needs not only can give you a sense of the seller's motivation level, but it can also help you to meet those needs.

I once dealt with a seller who began to buy non-apartment properties and had a nice one under contract. He wanted to do a 1031 exchange out of his apartment so he could defer his taxes from the proceeds. This was a sound strategy.

It was even better for me because I knew he had to sell his apartment by a certain date to meet the federal 1031 deadlines. That gave me an advantage. I showed him that I could perform the closing before his deadline; in return, I got the property for a bit less than market value.

I'm in a situation right now where someone wants to sell because he's got a new franchise business. It's going great, but is very cash-intensive. For him to grow this business and get more profits, he needs more cash to run operations. He's selling his property to get that cash. He might care more about a quick closing than about extracting every last dollar from me.

Sometimes, you won't find any pressing needs. It might be that the seller simply wants to cash out in the next few years and retire. Even though you can't appeal to an urgent need, you still can paint a picture for that seller of how nice it will be to get away from the headaches of property management.

This type of knowledge can only help the outcome of your negotiations.

3. Set Your Goals and Rank Them in Order of Priority

Of course, I realize you ultimately want cash flow and appreciation. But you must be clear on your more immediate goals when coming to the negotiating table.

A priority for you may be to close by a certain date. You may have a 1031 exchange you must complete by that date. If this is the case, do *not* let the seller know it during the negotiation process. If you do, the advantage goes to the seller.

Sometimes the primary goal is lowest price. Of course that's important, because if you pay too much, then cash flow becomes smaller as a percentage of purchase price.

For most beginning investors, price is not the primary goal: Let's say you want to get your first deal done, and you don't have a lot of cash. Your goal may therefore be to get into the deal for as little money out of pocket as possible. You may be willing to pay a little more if you can get seller financing for part of the purchase price. You might even have money for the down payment, but need the seller to pay closing costs.

Minimize Your Down Payment with These Tactics

If you want to get a chunk of cash at the closing table for your down payment, negotiate the closing date between the third and the seventh of the month.

When you do this, the rents will be prorated: The owner will have collected rents on the first and he is to give you rents equal to the remaining days in the month. If you close on the third, the seller will give you 27 or 28 days of rent.

Be careful: Some tenants will not have paid rent to the seller by the time your closing takes place. The seller may tell you that "the tenants are good for it." Don't fall for that! Tell the seller you want all the rent that is due you—meaning he must pay out of his pocket for missing rents—and because the tenants are "good for it," you'll be glad to forward the rent when you collect it.

You may have done your walk-through and realized the property will need some immediate repairs. Instead of having the money come out of your pocket for those repairs, ask the seller to give you a repair allowance.

This means the seller will give you money at closing for the repairs. If the seller says no, either take the hit or walk away. Decide by redoing the numbers: See if the deal works with the price inflated by the amount of the new repairs. If it does, then ask the seller to increase the price and give you that repair allowance.

This will not cost him a penny, because that money will be deductible as a closing expense and he will not be taxed on the difference in sales price amounts. Some sellers understand this and others don't. If your seller doesn't understand, or does not believe it will be deductible, ask whether your accountant can call his accountant.

Write down all your needs going into the deal. Then rank them in order of priority and work to get your primary need met first. Once you cross that one off your list, focus on the next one.

You don't necessarily have to negotiate them in the order you ranked them. Some of your more important goals may actually be easier to negotiate than others, depending on the seller's goals.

One or two of your goals may be deal killers if you don't get them. Mark them that way on your list up front, and stick to your guns. You may have to walk away. That's okay—we both know your marketing system will bring you more deals very soon.

4. Decide What Your Strike Price Is and Don't Exceed It

Speaking of holding firm, you must determine your maximum price, also known as the *strike price*. Then, you must not exceed it!

Do not try to determine this during negotiations. You must know it beforehand, when you are not emotionally involved with the deal. Sure you want it, but you also realize that at some price, it's no longer a good deal.

If you wait until the heat of negotiations, pressure can easily affect your judgment. When it looks like you may not be able to get the deal for the price you generally had in mind—because you didn't set a firm strike price—you now start to rationalize. You convince yourself that maybe you can stretch a little more and make the deal work at the higher price.

This usually takes the form of tweaking the numbers and using best-case scenarios for income or expenses. It's a fool's game. Don't be that fool.

It happens every day at auctions. In fact, it's why banks would rather auction off a property before putting it on the market to be sold. As bidding gets higher, excitement builds. The high bidder becomes the center of attention. Emotions completely overwhelm reason and many investors wait far too long before dropping out.

They also rationalize that because the people they are bidding against are willing to go higher, it *must* be a good deal. Those people are thinking the same about *you!*

Know your price and stick to it, and it will be one more sign that you're a pro.

5. ANTICIPATE THE NEXT MOVE AND DON'T AVOID HAGGLING

Negotiating is like playing chess. Always look at all your possible moves and analyze them one by one. If you move one piece a certain way, what would be your opponent's likely response? If you take a different approach, then what do you suppose your opponent is likely to do now? This should be part of your preparation.

Of course, you can't predict your opponent's moves with certainty. That's not the point. You should prepare as much as you can, and not use the excuse of "I won't try to predict, because I may be wrong."

Speaking of anticipating, you should expect to haggle a bit. You say you hate to haggle? I have two responses:

1. The right kind of haggling is actually helpful to both you and the person across the table from you.
2. Get over it.

I used to think: "I'll just state my best offer up front. That's the *honest* way to negotiate." Here's what would happen to me:

Me: "I'll give you $1.2 million for your property."

Seller: "I really can only take $1.6 million for it."

Me: "I understand your position, but I've run the numbers and I think I can only make it work at $1.2 million."

Seller: "Well, I may be able to take $1.4 million for it, if you're able to close quickly."

Me: "Oh, I can close quickly, but I'm afraid that $1.2 million is the best I can do."

Seller: "Hmmm—I don't see how I can realistically go below $1.4 million . . . but I like you. Tell you what: Let's split the difference and settle on $1.3 million and you have a deal."

Me: "I'm sorry, Mr. Seller, but I was honest with you right up front. The numbers only work for me if I can pay $1.2 million, so that's unfortunately all I can do."

Seller: "You know what? Forget the whole deal! I've been bending over backward to try to meet your price, and have dropped my price two times, and you haven't budged. That's not negotiating in good faith. The deal's off."

And the seller would be right to walk away! I gave him nothing to feel good about. Had I started at $1 million and come up to $1.2 million, he still might not have come down to there—but he *might* have. At least if he did, he could hold his head up high and tell himself (and his spouse): "We both gave in a little and met halfway."

Let's get rid of the bad, image-laden word *haggling*, and call it *positioning*. Take a position that gives you room to negotiate and ultimately makes the other person feel good about the transaction.

The same thing is true for less-important issues like who pays closing costs or smaller repair items. You should consider initially asking for concessions that you don't truly need. That allows you to sweeten your offer by caving in on these items. You may also have to cave on important stuff, but this gives you a little padding to absorb the blows.

6. Remain Calm and Unemotional

Our brains are wired to be at their best when we're alert but not agitated. The Goldilocks *Just-Right Principle* applies here: If we have too little interest and energy, the mental gears are not moving; if we're overstimulated, it's very difficult to think straight.

How many times have you been in a stressful situation and later kicked yourself, thinking: "It's so obvious to me now; why couldn't I come up with that response at the time!"

You'll negotiate with people from all walks of life, and some of them will be a pleasure to deal with. You don't need my advice for handling them. But when you come across a skilled negotiator, get prepared for some fireworks.

Some smart negotiators will *try* to make you feel uncomfortable. They'll do both subtle and blatant things to get you frustrated, angry, impatient, or all of the above. If they succeed, they know your judgment is now clouded and the advantage goes to them.

For instance, they may make you wait 20 minutes or more. Maybe they arrange for you to face a very bright window. During the conversation, they may continuously ask you to repeat yourself. Perhaps they constantly click a pen or jiggle a leg. Any of these behaviors could just be accidental; then again, that's how they're supposed to look.

They want you to focus on meaningless things and *not* on your strategy. Whether it's intentional or not, you must simply remain calm and unemotional throughout the negotiations. It will give you the clearest mind and the best chance of achieving your goals.

Your calm demeanor in the face of actual efforts to unnerve you may have the opposite effect: You might fluster the other party!

7. BUILD RAPPORT AND TRUST

Let's assume that you're not dealing with someone made of stone, but your seller is a regular person. You will increase your odds of success if you get the seller to like you first and trust you second. Most people prefer to do business with people whom they like and trust. That factor could win a deal for you in a competitive situation where price and other deal terms are fairly equal.

You get a seller to like you by establishing rapport, and you do that by finding something in common.

Remember the preparation you did in Secret Number One? You fished around by asking about the seller from the broker, lender, and anyone else in the transaction. You googled that person and went to the seller's web site, if one exists.

You're simply looking for clues like that person's alma mater, hobby, or any apparent interest. Notice what kind of car the seller drives up in. What do her clothes tell you about her?

You don't need to find these clues before the negotiations, though that's always helpful. Maybe you'll only learn halfway through that she's a big fan of Mexican food.

Whatever you can latch onto that you can say you also enjoy or admire, do it. Make it genuine.

That tiny common ground is all you need to begin a good relationship. Over time, this kernel of rapport can turn into trust.

When a seller likes and then trusts you, your negotiations will go much more smoothly. You'll both find it easier to give in on lesser issues to make the deal happen.

8. CREATE A WIN/WIN ENVIRONMENT

My goal in negotiating is not to stomp the other person into the dirt and emerge victorious. People have a way of getting back at you when they realize they've been railroaded into a bad deal. When you need to go back to them for some other detail of the transaction, you'll now find they're much less reasonable.

You should be in this business for the long term. You want your good reputation to spread like ripples on a pond after you close each deal. People love to gossip, and that gossip can be either "What a pro"—or "What a jerk."

I'm not suggesting that you cave in. Look instead to sign a deal that's fair for both parties.

A great way to start is to ask the seller—right up front—"What are your goals for this negotiation?" His answer will tell you how to negotiate with him. Sometimes, the first thing out of his mouth will not be price. It might be a quick closing or some other factor.

Let's just say it's "the highest price." Now you ask, "What do you consider the highest price to be?"

You may be surprised by the answers you get. Sometimes the seller will drop way below the original asking price just by your asking this question. On other occasions, a seller may say, "I want the asking price," or sometimes even more. *You must ask and not assume.* Then you'll have a basis for knowing that person's definition of a fair transaction.

9. Remain Flexible and Open to Options

Always negotiate with an open mind. If you go in with the idea that you'll only accept one outcome, you'll lose more deals than you should.

A fellow investor once negotiated on a piece of land on which he wanted to build apartments. He was stuck on getting that land for no more than $320,000, but the seller wanted $400,000. They were at an impasse.

Instead of walking away from the deal, the buyer decided to inspect the property one more time. He was firm on his strike price (see Secret Number Four), but wanted to see if there was any way to make additional money from the property. That would allow him to raise his strike price and still have the deal work.

Notice that he wasn't rationalizing a way to increase his strike price; he was inspecting the property to see if he missed something the first time around. This time, he noticed a very large mound of sand on the property that he must have ignored the first time through.

He took a sample to another contractor he knew and his second walk-through paid off: The sand was a special type that septic systems must use in his state. The pile of sand alone was worth $2 million!

He hightailed it back to the seller and decided he could find a way to pay $400,000 after all.

Of course, if you've shown flexibility and are still being asked to give in, you may reach a point where you must say "no." At that point, it's fine to explain that it's your final offer, and you must walk away from the deal if it can't be met.

If the seller doesn't budge, *make sure you walk away!* If you cave now, you just flushed your credibility. Do not say one thing and do another.

If you do walk away, it doesn't mean the end of the world. First, you know there are other deals coming through your pipeline. Second, you can go back to the seller later and give some reason why you'd like to continue the negotiations. You maintain your credibility because you did walk away for that particular session. After all, the seller may have had second thoughts too about not wanting the deal to fall through, and may welcome another opportunity.

10. When the Seller Speaks, Listen Closely and Delay Your Response

We all want to know we're being heard. Yet, many negotiators make the mistake of focusing on what they're saying, and not what the other party is saying.

They talk, and then, when the other person speaks, they don't listen. They put a blank mask on their face instead and are simply formulating what they'll say next.

Do this enough and you'll frustrate your opponent. The seller may begin to disconnect from the negotiations because he figures you're not listening. You'll just make matters worse if you jump in before the seller is finished.

Remember that you should be listening for clues, for unspoken motives, and for opportunities to establish rapport. You'll help your cause if you:

- Listen while making eye contact.
- Actually process what the seller is saying.
- Pause very briefly before speaking.

It shows that you're paying attention and are not merely rattling off a script. You may even discover something you can use!

11. Demonstrate Empathy

It's corny, but true: They don't care what you know until they know you care. You'll be a better negotiator if you show empathy with your seller.

A tried-and-true formula is called *feel, felt, found*. Weave these three words into some of your responses to sellers, and you'll notice positive reactions.

You might say: "I know how you feel about increasing the repair allowance; others have felt the same way. What they've found is that the repair allowance increased their depreciable cost basis and. . . . "

When you use this construction, it telegraphs that you're listening and respect the other person's position. It's the opposite of implying "You're crazy."

It also leads the seller to a solution. The part that goes: "This is what they found. . . . " helps the seller see how other people have successfully overcome whatever objection is on the table.

You can even use this technique in other settings, such as with co-workers or your boss (until real estate sets you free!). Two bits of advice though: Be genuine about the content you put into the technique; and don't overdo it. Remember, it's just *one* tool.

12. Silence Is Golden

Occasionally, less is more: Give your offer and then *shut up*.

Some people make their offer and immediately get nervous. If the seller doesn't respond right away, they may conclude their offer was too low. This is called *forecasting*.

You have no idea what the seller is thinking—and I know you can't read minds, or else I'd have seen you on the cover of *Time* magazine.

Some sellers respond as soon as you make your offer. Either their minds are quick to analyze offers, or else they're just using their *gut instinct.* Other sellers are slow to respond, for one reason or another.

I belong to the first category. My mind works quickly and I like to get similar responses from sellers. When I first found myself negotiating with people who liked to respond slowly, I took this as a sign that they didn't like my offer. Without their saying anything, I would then raise my offer closer to my strike price.

I made this expensive mistake until it finally dawned on me that their silence did not necessarily mean disapproval. I then made two rules for myself:

1. After making my offer, I'd just sit tight and say not one word until I'm *told* by the seller what his reaction to my bid is. I would no longer assume.
2. When I was the seller, I'd use this phenomenon to my advantage. I would now be the one to remain quiet when someone gave *me* a number. If I previously became anxious and silence made me sweeten my offer, maybe others would feel the same way.

Sure enough, it worked! As a buyer, I stopped needlessly raising my bid; as a seller, my silence tempted bidders to sweeten their offers.

Once in a while, you'll find yourself in a standoff. You'll make your offer and will go quiet . . . and wait . . . and still the other side says nothing! You will at first become uncomfortable, because people find the silence awkward and want to fill that vacuum.

There's an old rule in sales that the first person to break that silence loses. I've found that to be generally true. Therefore, if you're across the table from a clever negotiator, just stay silent, relax, and maybe even smile slightly. But do not speak.

I once was locked in a war of wills with someone, and the silence went on for about 10 minutes! Finally, I wrote the word "decission?" on a piece of paper and slid it over. The other person just couldn't stand it anymore, and said: "You spelled it wrong."

I said: "I know." He then realized what had just happened, and we both laughed. (As I recall, that turned out to be a good deal for me!)

Notice that none of these secrets is a *dirty trick.* They're all just recognizing human nature and using it to arrive at a *fair deal for both parties.* I suggest you review these 12 secrets regularly until they become second nature.

IN THE NEXT CHAPTER

It's easy to get the wrong idea about repositioning, and think it must be a mammoth project. Fortunately, there are tricks of the trade that really stretch your dollars.

We talked earlier about *buying right.* In the next chapter, I discuss how to *improve your property right,* so every dollar you invest comes back to you multiplied.

CHAPTER 10

The 80/20 Rule of Rehabbing

Who would have ever thought that a nineteenth-century Italian sociologist and economist would be relevant to your repositioning project? Well, he is, and his name is Vilfredo Pareto. He cooked up the *80/20 Rule.* Pareto noticed that 80 percent of something (in his case, wealth in Italy) is due to 20 percent of something else (in his case, a small group of wealthy people).

And so it is with your repositioning project: You will get 80 percent of the benefit from doing 20 percent of all the things you could do to reposition that property.

You must hit the *sweet spot* for maximum profit. If you under-repair a property, it won't attract the new tenant profile you're after. If you over-repair it, you'll get the tenants, but your *return on investment* drops, because it cost you more than it should have to attract those tenants.

I see people over-repair properties more than under-repair them. Of course, I'm not advocating that you leave things in bad shape because you may have a C– property and want to attract C+ tenants. I'm suggesting that C+ tenants will pay you C+ rents, and should therefore not get granite countertops.

Conversely, if you have a B property and plan to attract A tenants, then don't go cheap and just resurface the countertops; replace them.

I once walked a site with a contractor on a property I was repositioning. He showed me a problem: Years ago a piece of wood near each window had been removed and not reinstalled by lazy painters who were redoing the exterior. Water found a way in and was causing wood damage.

We are talking 1,500 windows here! He said the solution was to add another piece of wood to all the windows after replacing any underlying wood that *may* have been damaged.

I told him we should install a piece of aluminum flashing and replace any wood that *showed* signs of damage.

He argued that the replacement piece must be wood, and not aluminum, so it would look correct architecturally. He was right, but so was I: I told him I didn't care if it looked architecturally correct; I just wanted a solid job done. I favored aluminum. The difference in price was $65,000.

He told me he *really* liked his work to look a certain way and he wanted to be proud when he took people over to the complex to show them his handiwork.

I told him I *really* like my profits to look a certain way and wanted to be proud when I showed my family our bank account.

I didn't hire that contractor. Do not allow contractors to tell *you* how it's going to be done. It's your project and you're interviewing them for possible hire. After listening with an open mind to their opinions, you tell *them* how it's going to be done.

In a previous chapter, I talked about structural and environmental changes. In this chapter, I focus on cosmetic changes. It's those types of improvements that get your property rented, and thus boost your net operating income. And when your NOI goes up, so does the value of your property.

EXTERIOR IMPROVEMENTS

Here are the most common exterior cosmetic improvements.

Paint

To give the property an instant spruce-up, simply paint exterior surfaces that are already painted. It really does do wonders. Repair any damaged wood before you paint, or you'll just have to paint again soon.

If you're just painting trim, there is no better color than white. If you are painting the entire exterior, I suggest you change the color of the property to a nice, neutral one. If it's already a neutral color, make it a different one. This telegraphs to residents and the community that something new is happening at your property.

Repair Wood and Brick

If your property is a combination of brick and paint, be sure the color matches the brick! This can be tricky, so if you're not sure, ask for suggestions.

If your property has wood siding with extensive damage, you have a decision to make: Will you replace the existing wood with more wood, or will you install vinyl? Prices can vary widely in different parts of the country. Go with the most cost-effective choice.

Repair Roofs

The roof is one of the first things you should repair or replace if it needs attention. If the roof is leaking, you must stop any more damage from occurring, not to mention all the justifiable tenant complaints.

Here's another reason to repair roofs early: Roof work is dirty, and exterior walls will get scuffed with ladder marks and falling debris. Working from the top down will prevent this.

Improve Landscaping

Take it from a former landscaper: Landscaping improvements are a great way to improve the appearance of a property *fast.* There's no better way to bring a change of attitude to your property than to add brightly colored flowerbeds.

Don't stop at the flowerbeds, but also examine the shrubbery. Is it old or overgrown? Are some areas full and others bare?

Most often, you'll find old, overgrown shrubbery. If it's way overgrown, get advice on whether it can be trimmed back or must be removed. If possible, trim it because well-manicured, mature plants look great.

Focus on the trees: Old ones give a property maturity and stature—and sometimes root problems. One of the main causes of plumbing problems is roots getting into pipes. They can also wreak havoc with foundations, walkways, and sidewalks.

I really hate to take down trees but occasionally you have no option. Otherwise, it's like the tree's roots have tapped into your bank account, too.

If the trees can stay, then see whether they need trimming. Cut back limbs that touch a building or roof. If trees substantially block different views of the property, simply trim lower branches so you have a nice line of sight. It's called *raising the canopy*. A skilled *arborist*, or tree expert, will not harm the trees at all but will instantly make your property look a lot better.

Repair or Replace Signage

Signage is huge. Very quickly and at low cost, you can advertise to the whole community 24/7 that things are different at your property.

First make sure you change the name. Not sure what to call it? Go to loopnet.com and browse thousands of names at complexes around the country. Pretty soon you'll have a short list of candidates and can ask around for votes. Then either update the existing signage with your new name, or consider installing completely new signs, including one of those small landscaped areas at the entrance to the property.

Rehabilitate the Pool

If your property has a pool, would you swim in it right now? If the water isn't crystal clear or the pool walls and decking are not well-maintained, you must do something. As I mentioned in an earlier chapter, you must gauge what your competition is doing. If your desired tenant profile lives in properties with pools, then you need one. If not, then you could potentially get rid of the pool and all its maintenance headaches.

On the other hand, it's not that expensive to drain, resurface, and refill a pool that's otherwise structurally sound. Get some new pool furniture and landscaping in there and you might just have turned an eyesore into a powerful amenity with a *resort* feeling.

Reseal and Stripe Parking Lots

When you consider how large and prominent driveways and parking lots are, they really merit your attention. Here again, your contractor can help to judge the extent of repairs needed. Many parking lots simply need to be resealed.

Don't forget the striping! This can be a sore point for tenants. If parking is tight and one lazy tenant continually hogs two spaces with sloppy parking, the manager will hear a constant stream of complaints. Or tenants will just move out when they have the opportunity. Restriping can help to keep inconsiderate drivers semi-conscious of their ways.

Improve Drainage

Standing water must get your attention. Not only does it annoy tenants, but it contributes to mosquito and even flooding problems. Make sure your property manager and contractor report the condition of the property after a long rain and get any problems fixed.

It might be as simple as adding gutters or repositioning downspouts. Perhaps landscaping needs to be reconfigured so water can run off. Whatever you need to do, it's worth it.

Fix Broken Window Mechanisms, Screens, Glass, and Blinds

Pay particular attention to windows. They don't have to be gorgeous; but they must be mechanically sound and attractive. This includes blinds and shades, which can really detract from a property if not maintained.

By the way, never allow tenants to put up their own blinds, shades, or other window treatments! You must keep them uniform and in good working order. When you see a property with a hodge-podge of shades—including sheets covering the windows—that's a property in decline.

Fix or Improve Lighting

Good exterior lighting is crucial. First, a well-lit area deters crime. Criminals prefer to do their business in the shadows. When a place is well-lit, they get suspicious that people could be watching them, including undercover police taking pictures.

Criminals will break lights to maintain their shadowy haunts. If this happens, simply put a cage around the light. It drives them crazy.

I once owned a six-family in a very rough neighborhood. I bought that property and another six-family across the street. A friend bought the 12-family next to mine. We had the three drug houses on the street. We figured that because we owned them all, we could work together, get rid of the drug dealers, and make a lot of money.

The first thing we did—after asking the state and local police to work with us—was to install floodlights high on the buildings, illuminating the entire area.

This worked well, except for a blocked-off area between my six-family and my buddy's 12-family. The action now moved there, where dealers dealed and hookers hooked. When we installed floodlights there, they were *immediately* broken. We then put cages around them—and they shot them out with BB guns. We put double cages around them, and they must have shot at those babies a hundred times with no success!

Game over. Within six months we had the whole area cleaned up and the city thanked us! (Consider what it's like to have a grateful city government when you need to go before the planning board or building inspector on a future project.)

Good lighting also increases safety. If an area is gloomy and a tenant slips and falls, your insurance company will get a call.

Make sure all your lights are fluorescent, because they save energy. Also put them on photocells, which automatically turn off during the day.

INTERIOR IMPROVEMENTS

The age of your property will be a very good indicator of the magnitude of your improvements. When it's been 20 years since a property was built or substantially rehabbed, things start to break down: Water heaters, furnaces, air conditioning, and fixtures all will be candidates for repair or replacement.

Over the following five years you can count on needing to repair or replace a large percentage of original parts. Be sure to add

1 to 2 percent onto your repair and maintenance budget for properties of this age.

Let's look more closely at the typical improvements worth making inside.

Paint

Use neutral colors: off-white for walls, semi-gloss white for the trim. If you want to get a little extra rent, offer an *accent wall* for $20 more a month. This option allows them to choose one of several approved colors to put on one wall in the living room. It works!

Nothing sells better than a freshly painted apartment.

Upgrade Appliances

Are they a little worn and scratched up? That's okay for a C property, but not for a B or an A. The A tenants want stainless steel or the latest colors and surfaces. Believe it or not, those 1970s appliances in *avocado green* or *harvest gold* won't even do for a C anymore! (D's are okay with them, though, if they're still functioning, and they often are.)

Appliances sell apartments, so keep them looking good. Often a good cleaning or touching up will go a very long way.

Repair Cabinets

Cabinet doors are frequently made out of particleboard, which can peel apart at the bottom. Many repositioners think they must install a whole new set of cabinets. They must not be aware of *refacing*. Home improvement stores can show you a dizzying number of colors and styles. The whole look of the cabinets can be upgraded by just changing the part facing out.

Repair or Replace Countertops

Take a close look at them. Most B and C properties with countertop problems can be upgraded with a texture overspray. This is a type of super-hard paint that comes in different colors and patterns. They look great and are very inexpensive.

Don't try this in an A property, though. There, you must put in new counters if the old ones are worn *at all.*

Repair or Replace Tile or Linoleum

It's probably tile in an A property (or many other property types in southern Texas because tile is so cheap there). You may find tile in some B's but mostly it's *lino,* as we like to call linoleum. You'll find lino in all C properties.

If any of it does not look good, replace it. Flooring technology has come a long way, and even lino can now look just like wood. It can make your apartments stand out and look great!

Clean or Replace Carpet

I like to use carpet for as long as I can. You might say my best friend is the carpet cleaner. They really can save you a great deal of money in carpet repair or replacement. That's important because carpet replacement will be one of your biggest expenses.

It must look good for a tenant moving in but it does not have to be *new.* If you have shag carpet or a funky color, replace it. Look to replace it with a medium-dark color. It should be not so dark that the room looks gloomy, but definitely not so light that it shows every stain.

In my opinion, multi-colored brown carpets work very well to hide stains and look presentable for a long time.

Refinish Hardwood Floors

Hardwood floors are easier than carpet to maintain, and cheaper than replacing carpet when you must refinish the wood. They also look classy and people love them. Even that vinyl product I mentioned is a step up from many carpets.

If you have hardwood flooring, you will be able to attract tenants with allergies by telling them that your units are allergy-friendly with no carpeting. People who love carpets can still put area rugs on those floors.

Replace Faucets

Do not be cheap here! Inexpensive faucets are a maintenance headache, and end up costing you more overall. Get good ones that look distinctive and elegant. Here's my rule:

If the tenant has to touch it regularly, make it special.

Tenants will stay in your unit longer and won't even know why!

Replace Light Fixtures

This is another quick way to enhance the appearance of your units. When you take over an older complex, the lighting is often the original stuff. This means it was in style 20 to 30 years ago. No doubt, the fixtures also do not match.

I like to replace all the fixtures with *brass and glass*. They are inexpensive and make the place look great. I've also found that ceiling fans are a big draw, so if you can add them, do it. They cost not much more than a plain fixture, yet have more perceived value. That's smart repositioning!

Replace Mirrors

Most bathrooms in apartments are just big enough to fit a tub, toilet, sink, and vanity. Try to make this heavily used room look as big as possible because *kitchens and baths sell units*. An easy trick is to add a mirror. Don't go for the rinky-dink medicine cabinet ones. Instead get as big a mirror as the room will support—like 4 feet by 4 feet or even larger. It will magically make the room look far larger.

If you're improving a really small apartment, also consider adding a mirror to the living room, hallway, or elsewhere.

Upgrade Laundry Room

Keep the laundry room neat and clean at all times. Someone should be cleaning it *every single day*. All machines must be in good working order and wiped down. There should be no trash visible, even after lazy tenants leave their lint repeatedly. And make sure the room is well lit.

The laundry room can either be a valuable amenity, or be an eyesore that warms the heart of your competitors.

If you take over a property with older machines, make a deal with one of the national laundry services. They'll replace all the machines with brand-new ones, and will do all the servicing. They typically charge you 50 percent of the cash the machines bring in, but you pay for nothing. It's often a good deal.

How to Get the Most from Insurance Claims

Whenever you have a problem that's severe enough to warrant a claim to your insurance company, you absolutely must use *public adjusters.* They negotiate with your insurance company on your behalf to get the most money for your claim.

They carefully review your policy to make sure you get paid for everything you're covered for. It's the opposite of what insurance companies do: They will send their own adjusters to your site. It's their job to get you to agree to the *lowest* amount possible. Sometimes, they even get bonuses for doing this.

Most people quietly accept what insurance companies offer because they simply do not know better. Now you know why insurance companies can pay for all those expensive TV ads and high-rise buildings.

You'll pay your adjuster around 10 percent of what you settle for from the insurance company.

Let me give you an example of how valuable this can be: A three-family property of mine had a fire on the second floor. Fortunately, no one got hurt. I did my own estimate and figured it would cost me $8,000 to fix the damage. The insurance company asked me to settle for $12,000. I thought this was a great deal—until my adjuster got the insurance company to settle for $36,000!

I think he earned his 10 percent, don't you? Since then, every time I've had a substantial claim on a property, I've always called an adjuster and received top dollar for my claim.

I know this sounds weird, but I don't dread bad things happening to my properties as long as no one gets hurt. I know my adjuster will take care of me. Hey, I pay hefty annual premiums. I want my advocate to get for me only what's rightfully mine—however deeply buried it may be in those confusing insurance documents.

DEALING WITH CONTRACTORS

Here's the bottom line: You must *get everything in writing.* I discovered this the hard way. If it's not in writing, it will not get done.

When I started out, I didn't use contracts. I had that romantic misconception that a person's word was all I needed. I soon realized that what I would say—and what some contractors would hear or remember—were two very different things.

I started using a generic contract from a local trade association, and that helped. But I was still getting cheated by contractors. I began to add a new clause to the contract each time I got ripped off. At least I wasn't getting cheated the same way twice!

After three years, I finally got that baby to be iron-clad. It was like controlling a dog on a leash. Let's go over some of the more important clauses you must make sure are in there.

Contactor Pulls Permits

Make sure the contractor—not you—applies for all permits. This saves you time and money, and takes liability off you. After all, the contractor is supposed to be the one with the licenses, and should be answerable to building inspectors for all work done.

Broom-Swept Condition

I'm sorry if I over-generalize here, but most contractors are slobs. You must therefore make it a written requirement to leave the work area in *broom-swept condition* at the end of *every* day. If you don't do this, your property will quickly become a mess. It can also become a hazard, with nails and tools left around. Building inspectors can be left with either a good or bad impression of workmanship, and I insist that it be a good one. I've fired contractors because they refused to keep the site clean.

Make sure the property looks its best at all times, especially because you'll be leasing or preleasing units while the work is being done.

Penalty Clause

This is the *mother of all clauses.* One of the biggest complaints I hear about contactors is they don't get the job done on time. It's true that if one contractor finishes late, he can throw off the schedule for several others.

Delays mean extra carrying costs for you, while units are empty. Contractors must finish on time, and if they don't, they must pay the price—literally. Add a penalty clause in all your contracts.

Ask contractors what is the longest possible time it could take them to do the job, and then put that date in the penalty clause. The penalty should be $50 to $200 per day for every day they go over the penalty date. The smaller the job, the smaller the penalty.

They can't argue too much: They chose the date. Set up all your contractors in this manner and then fill in your job schedule. This one clause will be the reason why your jobs come in on time, and your competitors' jobs won't.

If you think contractors will just balk at this clause, I have news for you:

1. I'm a contractor, so I know how they think.
2. I've used it successfully for years.
3. The ones that balk are the ones you don't want anyway.
4. Contractors who know the work and are professionals will respect what you're doing. After all, they'll realize that with this clause in place, *other* subcontractors on your job won't cause the whole schedule to slip for everyone else.

Scope of Work

This clause spells out in writing specifically what the job will require. And it must be very specific. If a contractor extracts extra money from you during the job, it will be because you weren't specific enough.

Make sure you include everything in the scope of work, because the contractor will be looking for what you miss. For example, is a Dumpster needed to remove debris from the site? Your scope of work should include a Dumpster that's provided by and removed by the contractor at his expense.

If it's not in your scope of work, the contractor sees this as an opportunity: He'll not provide it, and will ask when you're planning on putting the Dumpster on site. At that point, you might say, "Hey, I assumed that was *your* responsibility!"

You're right: You assumed it, and you now are going to pay for it. This happened to me early in my career. Do you see how much money and trouble you will save yourself, all because you bought my book?

Draw Schedule

After you get the *scope of work* done, break it down into a *draw schedule.* This tells each contractor when he will be paid, and what work must be completed for him to get paid.

Never give contractors 50 percent up front and 50 percent at the finish! If you do, you most likely can kiss that money goodbye. It should instead be 10 percent/30 percent/30 percent/30 percent. With 10 percent up front, the contractor can buy materials; then after each 30 percent of the work is complete, you (actually, your construction supervisor) will inspect the work and send another check to the contractor.

If some contractors insist on getting 50 percent up front, what they're really doing is using that money to finish up *another* job. Or they may simply want to get as much cash as possible up front, because most owners don't know to push back.

If they simply won't do the job unless you put up a big initial deposit, go on to the next contractor.

When your contractors do the work, remember to *pay them quickly* and you'll be rewarded with even better service.

Punch-Out List

When a contractor completes 30 percent of the work and requests a draw release, you *must* inspect the property to be sure all the work for that phase is complete. Bring your scope of work and draw schedule, both of which were signed by you and the contractor.

Walk the site with the contractor, checking off the items that are done. If it's 100 percent complete, cut a check *on the spot.* He will love you for that.

If it's not complete, turn to him and say: "Mr. Contractor, we both agreed that all these items had to be complete for you to be paid. I've marked on this *punch-out sheet* the items that are not complete. Once they're done I can cut that check. Please sign the punch-out sheet."

Change Orders

Once in a while something will come up on a job, and no one saw it coming. Maybe it was the discovery of *ledge* (solid rock) when a septic system was being installed; maybe it was unusual framing when a wall was opened up—whatever the surprise, the job just changed.

Before the work begins, you need a clause in the contract covering *change orders.* It must state that for the contractor to get paid for any extra work done, that work must be spelled out in a change order form and must be agreed upon between you and the contractor. The change order form must be signed and dated *before the extra work begins.*

This is a key clause, and here's what will happen if you don't use it: At the end of the job, your contractor will hand you two bills: One for the last 30 percent disbursement from the disbursement schedule, and another for the extra work that was completed on the site.

Now you must haggle with the contractor and either pay all, some, or none of it. If you pay none of it, you risk having the contractor file a *mechanics lien* on your property. It could prevent you from reselling it until the lien is removed. Both you and the contractor may know you're right, but that won't matter. He's calculating how much you're willing to spend in time and legal fees versus just paying him off. Too bad, when you could have avoided the whole mess by using a change-order clause.

Home Address and Telephone Number

Your contractors should know that you know where to find them. This is a deterrent from their pulling any funny business.

When I get the address and number, I always call the house during working hours in hopes of speaking with the spouse. I simply tell the spouse how excited I am to have the contractor working for me.

Of course when the contractor comes home, the spouse reports that "Dave called." This reaffirms in the contractor's mind that I know how to find him if necessary.

Lien Waiver

Every single time you pay contractors, get a *lien waiver* that waives their right to file a lien on your property relating to that portion of their compensation. If you don't—as discussed earlier—you risk having the contractor file a lien in the future so he can extract more money from you.

Don't ever pay contractors in cash, *regardless of the discount they give you.* If you do, you may be surprised to find a lien waiver on your property for the amount you paid them in cash! How will you then prove that you paid them?

Fudge Factor

Remember what I talked about in an earlier chapter: The two main reasons why repositionings go bad is *lack of money* and *bad management.* Therefore, don't go into a repositioning unless you can build in a cushion of 10 to 20 percent on improvement expenses. This is your *fudge factor.*

After you get bids from all contractors, review those bids and figure out how much it will cost you to do the whole job. After you select the winning bids, always add 10 to 20 percent of the entire improvement cost.

If you're just starting out, make it 20 percent. If you've done a few projects already, add at least 10 percent, or more if your experience dictates. Very rarely does a job come in at or under budget, so don't bet the viability of your entire project on that happening.

If you don't need the cushion, great! You have extra money. If you do, you've used it as a hedge to make sure your repositioning crosses the finish line and you are rewarded for your work.

Without all these clauses and practices—every one of which I learned the hard way—contractors are in control of you and much of your bank balance. With the clauses in place, it's *you* who is in control.

IN THE NEXT CHAPTER

Most investors are scared stiff to invest in apartments because they don't want to become janitors and bill collectors to their tenants. These investors simply don't understand the ins and outs of using property managers to do all that.

Once you know how to find, hire, and manage the professionals who in turn manage your properties, you become liberated! Read on and discover how property managers can free your time and help grow your portfolio quickly.

CHAPTER 11

How to Avoid Being a Landlord: Secrets to Hiring Great Property Managers

I'm actually glad that there's so much bad information out there about apartment investing. I know it sounds mercenary, but the more investors who buy wrong, burn out, and sell at a discount to me, the happier I am.

Landlords have no one to blame but themselves. They think they know it all, so they don't take the time—the way you are right at this moment—to find out the right way to invest in apartments. Then they deal with tenants and repairs because either they don't know any better, or they're too cheap to hire someone.

Don't *you* fall into that trap of becoming a *landlord!* Landlords deal with tenants, trash, and toilets. Investors deal with tennis, travel, and Tahiti!

As an investor, you should look at this business through the eyes of a CEO. Even if you're the only person in your new real estate investing business, you're still the CEO. That gives you three responsibilities:

1. Grow the business.
2. Create cash flow.
3. Cash checks.

If your business is not growing, it's stagnant or in decline. If you are not moving forward, your competition is getting ahead of you.

You may have heard this: Every morning the lion wakes up in the jungle and knows he's got to run faster than the slowest gazelle or he'll starve. Every morning the gazelle wakes up and knows that to survive, he's got to run faster than the fastest lion. Either way, you had better wake up and get running!

Next, you should focus on creating cash flow. It's the lubricant that makes your business engine run. Without it, your obligations would soon grind everything to a halt.

Lots of businesses show profits or assets on paper, but go *four-legs-in-the-air* because of a lack of cash flow. When you manage your apartment business properly, you'll never be short of tenants working all month long to send you 30 percent or so of their earnings in the form of cash.

Finally, as your business begins to thrive, you get the happy task of cashing the monthly checks that represent profit after all expenses are paid. You deserve this reward for all your smart decisions.

If you focus on doing the maintenance on your apartment buildings, you will end up making a maintenance worker's wages. If you act like the CEO of your business and delegate the management, you'll make a CEO's wages. It's your call.

I'd like to share with you a revelation I got in my second year as an investor. I have always been into fitness and I regularly work out. I like to meet with a group of people at 5:00 A.M. so we can get our workouts in. At that hour, the gym is empty and you get to know the other die-hards pretty well.

One guy had a corporate job in finance and worked under a chief financial officer. He came in one morning and told us the CFO had just lost his job and wouldn't be replaced. They'd instead use my friend and another person as co-replacements but had no plans to elevate them to the CFO position.

My friend didn't have a problem with this, because he was hoping for a nice bonus from part of the CFO position salary of $135,000. It didn't work out that way.

I asked him how old the CFO had been; he said 52. At that moment, I knew I had made the right choice in investing in real estate. At the time I was 31, had been in real estate for 2½ years, and had made over $300,000 the previous year!

Here's the best part: I didn't have to rely on anybody else to give me a raise. No awkward performance reviews and hoping that the company as a whole did okay. No getting out a magnifying glass to see the bonus pool. I gave myself raises by buying new properties. My review consisted of looking at my financial statements, which steadily got better. That's what real estate can do for you, too.

Be an investor and leave the landlording to someone else who's okay with it and doesn't have the big goals and dreams that you do.

HOW TO FIND THE BEST MANAGERS

Where do you find the best managers? In my previous book, *Emerging Real Estate Markets*, I introduced you to the *Institute of Real Estate Management*. This organization trains managers and owners of management companies in the best practices of real estate management.

Participants earn designations by taking a series of classes and passing tests at the end of each course. The entire process takes between one and four years to complete to earn one of two designations: Certified Property Manager (CPM) or Accredited Residential Manager (ARM).

CPMs handle the bigger properties and ARMs handle the smaller ones.

The best thing about this resource is you can go online to irem.org and put in any city in the United States. All the CPMs and ARMs in that city will come up with their full contact information. If you don't live in a city that has CPMs or ARMs, then broaden your search area. There will usually be some in a nearby city.

I like to get two or three names and interview them. Even though these are the cream of the crop when it comes to property management, I still want the best of the best. I ask them a series of questions and am looking for particular answers.

I ask, of course, how long they've been in the business. They should have been successfully managing *your type* of property for at least five years.

I then ask for some of those addresses where they've been managing and check out those properties. I'm looking for two things:

I look at how well the exterior is maintained. This is not so much for deferred maintenance, because the owner may be too cheap to pay for repairs. I'm instead focusing mainly on overall cleanliness, over which the manager has total control.

I'm also looking for the management sign. Each management company has a sign with its name and logo. Remember that sign, and as you drive around town, look for it on other buildings. You'll get a good idea of what their properties really look like.

I always ask: "What is your tenant retention policy?" As I mentioned in an earlier chapter, they should be able to go on for 10 to 15 minutes about all the things they do to keep tenants in the building. If they don't, that's a red flag.

I want to know how long it takes for a typical unit to be made ready after a tenant moves out. The faster it's done, the sooner I'm making money with a new tenant. A typical turn takes three days. If an apartment has extensive damage, it will naturally take longer.

I want to hear their marketing plan: Tell me how they'll keep my units full and keep that cash flow coming. They should be able to give you seven or eight actions they regularly take to attract new tenants.

I want to know if the maintenance will be done by their staff or by hiring out to contractors. It's much more expensive to hire out. If it is being done by the staff, I want to know what the hourly wages will be, because I'm the one who ultimately pays them. I'll later determine whether that is market rate or not.

Ask for references and call them.

Ask if they have been sued at any time in the last five years and for what. The presence of a lawsuit does not necessarily indicate a problem, because *slip-and-fall* cases from tenants are common. But I'm looking for patterns, and also for who is suing: If the prior owners filed suit, I want to know the details.

Always ask if they provide their managers with any type of special training. Bigger management companies have their own in-house training programs, and they put their people through them regularly. Smaller companies should send their staff to courses at the Institute of Real Estate Management or at the National Apartment Association.

You should ask to interview the proposed on-site manager. This is a key person on your team. Even though you probably won't often talk with the manager, you do want to get a feel for this person.

Ask the management company if it will provide a written management plan for the property. This is equivalent to a business plan. If it won't commit to a plan in writing, find another company. This plan should contain the company resume, a marketing plan, and a five-year projected profit-and-loss statement.

The management plan contains the marketing plan, which will tell you how they will keep your property full. If their main marketing technique is to use relocation services, find another management company.

Relocation services and classified ads are the two most expensive ways to get tenants into your building. That's no marketing plan. You should insist on a comprehensive one with multiple approaches, both higher- and lower-cost.

Management companies vary in their fees for attracting new tenants. Ask up front what they'll charge up front. For smaller buildings (2 to 20 units), they may charge you from 50 to 100 percent of one month's rent for each new tenant they deliver.

Properties from about 16 to 50 units can support a resident manager, who does the marketing, manages tenants, and does much of the maintenance. Sometimes the management company will also enlist the support of other staff to help the resident manager.

From 50 to 100 units, you'll have a site manager. This person may or may not live at the property, but definitely is responsible for all aspects of your property. There also will be a part- or full-time maintenance person.

At 100 units, you will have enough cash flow to afford a manager and a leasing agent. This makes both the lease-up and overall management of the project a lot easier.

The leasing agent is usually paid hourly and gets a bonus for each lease brought in. The typical bonus is $25. If you are doing a repositioning and need to lease up many units quickly, then pay more. Incentives work.

Before hiring the management company, it's a good idea to do some *mystery shopping*. Get the names of properties managed by that company, and then visit a couple of them. Pretend you're moving into town and are looking for an apartment. How aggressively does the manager or leasing agent try to close you? Is the person half-hearted and just wishes you'd go away? Or do you have a motivated manager who asks you several times if you're ready to fill out the application?

You should be asked at least three times. Then after you decline and walk away, you should get a follow-up phone call within 48 hours.

While you're there, check out whether the office is tidy, and what the staff is wearing.

Good leasing offices will have a tray of cookies or popular snacks to give prospective tenants. It's called the *Law of Reciprocity*. If I give you something, you'll have a conscious or unconscious urge to give me something in return. (Why do you suppose charities send you address labels?) Good marketers swear by this technique.

In one of our properties in San Marcos, Texas, we've got an Otis Spunkmeyer™ cookie machine. Fresh cookies are pumped out all day, and people love them!

What You Should Expect to Pay

When negotiating with the management company, this is one time when you shouldn't try to strike too hard a bargain. Find out the average rate in your area for properties your size and just pay it.

Always calculate rates as a percentage of gross collected rents or total revenues for the month. The more money they bring you, the more money they'll make.

Some management companies tell you they have a minimum amount you must pay; that's baloney. What they are really telegraphing to you is if (when?) they don't perform, they still want to be paid.

For 2 to 30 units, expect to pay 10 percent of gross collected rents. From 30 to 100 units, the average is 5 to 6 percent of gross collected rents. From 101 to 250 units, it's 4 to 5 percent. Anything over 100 units will be from 3 to 4 percent of gross collected rents.

Recordkeeping

If they still use log books and are not on the computer with current management software, then let them stay in the Stone Age and move on to another company.

If they have computerized records, ask for sample reports and have them explain the reports to you. The very best is when you have Internet access to your property reports so you can get real-time results of your property any time you want.

Marketing Budget

Ask what the budget will be to keep your units full. If your property is on a main road, it will be easier to fill your units and costs should be less. People will literally be coming off the street to rent your units. In fact, this type of easy access is definitely something you should look for when buying a building.

As I said earlier, the marketing plan should be diverse, with lots of action items that don't cost much: Contacting local businesses, handing out flyers, and putting up a web site are three good ones. I just heard that around 30 percent of all applicants are now coming from the Internet.

Banner signs in front of the property are very effective. Combine them with open houses and the property will get a lot of attention.

Tenant Screening

Ask who will perform the tenant background checks and what they charge. Many national companies will screen tenants for credit and crime history. Whatever they charge, you should get at least that amount in an application fee, if not more.

You must decide who will qualify to come into your building. For instance, what will be your requirement for income as a multiple of rent? Most A and B properties require income to be three times the rent. In C properties, the average is 2.5 times the rent.

Then decide on the minimum credit score you will allow. Finally, you must decide which crimes you will allow people to have in their background and still get approved for rent.

In a fantasy world, you can say "zero crimes and high credit rating." In the real world we live in, you'll have to balance these factors against your vacancy rate and how many people are applying to live in your property.

If you're hurting for tenants, you either must accept lower-quality ones or reposition that property higher. It's all a matter of supply and demand.

I remember when I first started buying apartment buildings in Brockton, Massachusetts. These were all C or C– properties. *Everyone* we screened had crappy credit, so we stopped looking at the credit reports. Many of our tenants (or someone in the immediate family) had some sort of criminal record. If we had been strict about *only the best*, we would have had empty buildings.

I decided to take people whose income was at least 2.5 times the rent, and who hadn't been evicted in the last five years. If they had been evicted in the last five years, that told me they knew how to play that game. If five years had passed and they hadn't been evicted from a property (but had been earlier), I figured they had learned their lesson.

This method worked well for me and continues to work well in that particular area. In other cities around the country where I invest, I am a lot stricter.

Follow This or Suffer the Consequences. Here's the deal about tenant screening: Whatever criteria you choose, that's okay—*as long as you use the same criteria for everyone walking onto that property*. You can even have different criteria for different properties. But you absolutely must use the same criteria for every applicant at a given property.

If you don't, you will be discriminating. Not only is that not ethically correct, but it will cost you a lot of money! The government has an active program of sending people out to visit and call properties. The little old lady or college student you just turned down might be a *Fed* who works with another type of person you just accepted. Do not even think of discriminating at your property if you want to stay in this business for long.

Avoid This Clause

Ask the management company if it will require you to list the property with it at resale. This clause is sneaked into many management agreements. When you use a real estate broker to sell your property, you don't want to be surprised to discover that you owe the management company a commission, too!

It's a management company and not a brokerage company. When I've taken that clause out of contracts, some management companies tell me the real money is in the sale. They are managing the property for that big sale payday, and if they can't have part of the sale it's not worth their while to manage.

When I hear this, I politely suggest they should open a brokerage business and get out of the management business. I want the option to use whomever I want to sell that property. If they have done an exceptional job managing, I will certainly consider using them for the resale. I refuse to award them that right up front. If that is not acceptable, that's just too bad.

Make Sure You Have Access to Your Money

Read that management agreement thoroughly. Make sure you are one of the authorized signers on all of your bank accounts. You'd be surprised at the number of management companies that do not want you to have signing authority on bank accounts where they are keeping *your* money.

This is a big mistake. Something may happen with that company: It may not perform, or it may actually do something detrimental to the property. In either case, you must have the ability to sever ties quickly and not have that company hold your bank accounts hostage.

The management company may object that they've had problems with owners in the past who drained the accounts and left the management company with past bills they had to pay. This is a valid concern for the management company, but it's not *your* concern.

I have a friend who used a management company that suddenly stopped performing. The property stopped throwing off cash and was in jeopardy of not being able to pay its bills.

My friend fired the management company, but could not get at the bank accounts. He had to take the company to court, and eventually won—after six months!

Length of Contract

Never sign a one-year contract without the option to get out of it in case of nonperformance. Both sides should have the ability to give the other a 30-day notice that it is canceling the contract.

I bought a 192-unit property that needed to be repositioned. I hired what appeared to be a qualified management company.

After three months, it was apparent that she was not doing her job. Even worse, she was *fudging*—you could say *cooking*—the books.

This is a cardinal sin. When your management company starts sending you false figures, one foot of your property is in the grave and the other is on a banana peel. All your decisions are based on these numbers.

In the case of my property, there happened to be an honest employee within the management company. She wouldn't take part in the lies and, as they say, *dropped a dime* on the crook.

We would have found out eventually. The bank deposits would not have matched what she was reporting to us. Still, the employee did us a favor and saved us a couple of months of trying to figure out what was going on.

Within 24 hours, we drained all operating accounts and opened new ones. We had all locks changed and our attorney sent her a cease-and-desist order. We established direct contact with the personnel we did want to keep, and it was over. She didn't know what hit her and we were able to protect our asset because we gave ourselves that option going into the contract.

Keeping Communication Lines Open

During the interview, ask for cell phone numbers. You must be able to reach your local manager when you have a problem or important question.

Perhaps you are concerned about a report you just received, or you heard about bad weather conditions in the area. If they won't give you the cell phone numbers of all staff related to your property, you have to wonder why: Is there a history of bad performance, and property owners continually called those cell phones? Regardless of their response, the only acceptable one is "Here's a complete list of cell phone numbers."

Now the Selling Starts

After asking all of these questions, you're just getting started! Now move to the questions that require them to *sell themselves*.

A good general one is: "Why should I use your company?" If they can't sell me into using their company, how are they going to sell a tenant into my units?

I then ask: "Describe your weaknesses to me." If this is the first time they've been asked this question, you'll see them squirm.

Don't let them get away with saying they can't think of any. Say you will give them another minute to think about it, because nobody's perfect and surely they can think of something. Then *go silent and wait.* Do not relieve the pressure. They will come up with something after a while. The smart ones respond with a hidden strength like, "I work too many hours making sure that everything is right with my properties, and my life tends to get out of balance."

I actually got that response, and this manager turned out to be excellent. (I can't vouch for her personal life, though.)

Finally, ask for three references of other owners that have used their services in the past or are currently using them. Call them.

No, you won't get just happy answers. If you try to keep the conversation going for a few minutes, you'll get 'em warmed up. You still might hear positive things, but occasionally someone will come out and say: "I want to be truthful with you . . ." and will then cut loose on everything the management company did wrong.

I had someone say: "I can't *believe* they gave you my number; I'm suing them right now!"

When you do get good references, then say: "Everything you told me sounds great, but no company is perfect. If you could improve the performance, what would you change?"

This will help you to prepare more questions for the management company because no one is, in fact, perfect. You want to focus mainly on strengths, but you definitely should be aware of any weaknesses up front.

REPOSITIONING MANAGERS: A SPECIAL BREED

Even if you've found a management company that has passed all the many tests I've just thrown out, you're still not done. If you're doing an apartment repositioning, that company—and the specific manager of your property—must have experience in this specialized field.

Let's go back to the two main reasons repositionings fail.

First Reason Why Repositionings Fail

Investors run out of money. They didn't take into account how much it would cost to get the entire job done.

In most cases, repairs come in over budget by at least 10 percent. If you are just starting out, add a 20 percent *fudge factor* into the repair numbers, as we discussed earlier.

Even if you nail the repair number and come in under budget, you could be off in regard to the schedule. You want both *under budget* and *on time*. What does a late schedule cost you? It's the revenue you missed by not having all units filled for that extra period.

Therefore, assume that contractors will take longer than they told you they would. I can't give you a specific number of months to assume, because it depends on the magnitude of the work. But another 10 percent or 20 percent fudge factor here would make sense.

Your next concern is the lease-up. How long will it take to:

- Get rid of the slow-payers, non-payers, and criminals
- Fix and fill the vacant units
- Increase occupancy to your breakeven point

It's critical that you get to breakeven as soon as possible. This is when that property stops bleeding and should soon be profitable. If you underestimate how long it takes to get to this point, you may not have the extra funds to cover your expenses beyond it. What a shame to come this far and now have to bail out just before the real money starts flowing!

Second Reason Why Repositionings Fail

Owners choose the wrong management company. (As I said earlier, if you chose to manage your first couple of repositionings yourself, you definitely chose the wrong management company!)

A management company gets paid two ways: a regular management fee to manage the complex, and a construction fee for managing the construction.

The construction fee will be between 5 and 10 percent of the construction cost. If you have a project that will cost $100,000 to repair, and a 10 percent construction management fee, you're looking at a total of $110,000 for the project.

A management company must be able to separate the property operations from the construction and repairs that are going on. Ask to see samples of the separate reports.

A common mistake is using maintenance people to help with construction repairs. Shortsighted or cheap managers do this. The result: deferred maintenance, leading to tenant discontent and lower revenues.

Keep your maintenance and construction staffs separate. After all, the management company is collecting two fees for these two different functions.

Daily Accountability Is Key

Construction will go much more smoothly if the management company insists on daily accountability from all contractors and subcontractors.

As you no doubt know, contractors are notorious for showing up at properties maybe three days out of the week. Sometimes, even that is optimistic. It's the manager's job to keep after them constantly to show up at the site and get the work done on schedule.

Each morning, the manager should walk the job with the contractor. They'll inspect the previous day's work to ensure it was done properly. Then they'll discuss what's on the agenda for the current day.

If this is done daily, your manager will discover problems early and can take corrective action before it gets much more expensive.

Take it from someone who's a licensed contractor and has managed hundreds of construction jobs: Daily accountability is the most often ignored, yet most effective form of construction management.

Choosing the Construction Company

Should you go with the big firm or the small one, the local guys or the regional outfit?

In my experience, go with a bigger company. They are usually more competitive because of *economies of scale:* They buy in bulk, and have more sophisticated systems that squeeze savings wherever possible. Also, if you need to get something done very quickly, it can pull more resources from other sites and get your job done.

The small outfits are okay too, but if you're on the fence between two good proposals, go with the bigger operation.

Big doesn't necessarily mean *national:* I almost always use local companies when I hire contractors. They know the market and the best suppliers. They may even know my property. When called back to make repairs, they are more likely to show up and get them done quickly.

How to Get Contractors to Beg You for Business

Considering how difficult it is to find good contractors, when you find one, I have some advice for you: Drop to one knee, pull out the ring, and start the wedding ceremony right away!

Fortunately, it's easy to keep them coming back to work with you: *Pay them on time.*

If they must chase you for money, the good ones will not come back to do the next job. If you pay promptly, but *nickel-and-dime* them, they're history.

Conversely, if you pay on time, you are separating yourself from the pack yet again (just as you are doing with brokers and all other members of your team). The contractors will not only show up when you have more work, but they'll drop everything when you call with an emergency.

Word-of-mouth works here, too: These good contractors know other tradespeople. When you treat them right, they'll refer other quality people to you.

When I started out many years ago, I asked my mentor what was the key thing he did right when *he* started out. The advice I just gave you was his answer.

What You Must Have from Your Contractor

Always make sure you get the contractor's license, insurance certificate, and workers' compensation certificate.

Only use licensed contractors for major projects and ones that require a permit. These people are licensed by the state and that means they've had to pass certain competency tests.

Some owners and managers use a lot of unlicensed contractors because they want to save money. Never do this with an electrician!

An incompetent electrician can burn down your property. Sometimes the poor quality work is a time bomb: It could be years later that stresses or corrosion finally take their toll and a couple of wires melt. Try tracking down the contractor then.

Even with licensed contractors, make sure they have liability insurance. If some contractor-related incident happens, you need to be reimbursed. Contractors tend to leave things lying around, and sometimes these things can hurt people. If that happens and the contractor doesn't have insurance, the lawyers are coming after you.

It's the same principle with workers' compensation insurance: One of the contractor's employees—or even the contractor himself—might get hurt on the job. If he isn't carrying workers' compensation insurance, you will become the target for compensation. These types of claims are usually very expensive.

MANAGING THE MANAGER: REPORTS YOU SHOULD GET REGULARLY

You should get this first report weekly: I call it the *Monday morning report* because that's when you should receive it. This report contains every key activity that happened the previous week for a given property.

Your current occupancy is at the top of the page. It's always nice to see your property at 95 percent occupancy or higher; this means you can increase rents.

The next item is the critical indicator of *traffic.* It's the number of people who either called or walked into the property, inquiring about renting an apartment.

Without traffic, you cannot lease your empty units. Especially when you own larger properties, every month you'll have units that must be filled. Even at 100 percent occupancy, you must fill units. It may be due to someone getting married, dying, or just moving out of town. Whatever the reason, you must be screening prospective tenants now to fill that next vacancy.

Under the traffic count number, you should see the *conversion rate,* which is the percent of traffic that results in a tenant moving in.

An average conversion rate is 33 percent, meaning one third of all traffic should be converted to preleased tenant status. If the number is higher, you've got a very good manager or leasing agent. If the number is lower, you must consider more training of staff. If the rate continues at a lower number, it's time to let the person go.

Your next number is *preleased occupancy*. This is where you'll be when all preleased units are full. If you are in a positive trend, your preleased occupancy will be above your current occupancy, taking all pending move-outs and move-ins into consideration.

If your preleased occupancy is below current occupancy, it's a warning sign. You're going to be losing ground soon.

You must be monitoring your occupancy exposure 90 days out. Your manager should be proactive in reviewing which tenants will have leases expiring and how desirable those tenants are versus the target profile. Then management takes the appropriate action.

Offer some sort of incentive to persuade tenants to stay. Perhaps it is steam-cleaning the carpets, installing ceiling fans, or replacing an older appliance.

When your manager makes this offer, tenants should give some indication of their intentions to stay or leave. Make sure your lease requires tenants to give you notice 60 days before they move. With 60 days, your manager can plan ahead.

The next line on your Monday morning report will be the number of notices coming due. Below that you should have the number of preleased units. There should be more pre-leased units than notices so you can keep occupancy up. If this is not that case, it's time to crack the whip and get your manager out there marketing more intensively.

Another important variable on this report is the amount of collections that have taken place. There should be a line with the total amount of rent that *could be* collected if all occupied units paid; below that should be the total amount that *has been* collected.

If you're into the third week of the month and 50 percent of your rents are still outstanding, you're in trouble. You must crack the whip again and get those managers out knocking on doors and making phone calls.

By the beginning of the third week, you should have 80 to 90 percent of rents collected. By the end of the month, your managers should have collected 97 to 99 percent.

If this is not the case, they are not doing their job. Sure, occupancy is great; but if the occupiers are not paying, what good is that?

The last line of the report shows *economic occupancy*. This is the percent of people who are living in your property and who are also paying. It would be nice for this number to equal your current physical occupancy, although it very rarely does. It's usually three to five points behind. The proximity of this number to your physical occupancy is a good indicator of how well or poorly the managers are doing their job.

Profit-and-Loss Statement

This monthly report gives you a detailed account of all revenue that came into the property, the sources of revenue, and all operating expenses. When the two are netted against each other, you arrive at *net operating income, or NOI.*

The goal is always to have NOI rising from the previous months. This means the property is consistently increasing in value.

The profit-and-loss statement (also known as the *P&L*) should be on the same page as the budget. The numbers and categories should be side by side so you can easily see how the property performed compared to the budget. The manager should explain in a *variance report* any item that varies from the budget by 10 percent—either negatively or positively.

Executive Summary

That variance report is often part of an *executive summary*. Management writes this report to give you a snapshot of overall property health. It should explain operations in regard to revenues, expenses, work performed, management issues, staff changes, and any other significant issues that have arisen in the last month.

The *rent roll* should be included in the executive summary. It backs up all the numbers being accounted for in the budget.

Budget

During the last quarter of each year, management should give you next year's budget for your approval. Look over that budget thoroughly. Be sure you understand and agree with these numbers as a realistic plan for operations.

- Is the management company being too optimistic?
- Are they running the property too lean?
- Are they doing just the opposite and padding expenses?

You'll make that determination when you review the budget.

One key method is to compare projected numbers to historical ones from last year. What were known issues last year, and how did those numbers turn out? Where do you think they could have saved you money? Where do you think they overspent?

Now compare last year's numbers to the budget for next year: Do you see a smooth trending, or are there anomalies? Put your thoughts, reactions, and questions on paper and use them as the basis for discussing the budget for next year.

YOU'RE AN ASSET MANAGER

Notice that in all the management details, I never suggested that you have direct contact with your tenants. I'm not saying to avoid it at all costs, but to put that job squarely on the shoulders of your managers instead.

Your job is to look at the numbers, manage the managers, and make decisions.

If the numbers tell you that your property is running smoothly, then *high fives* to everyone involved. If the numbers tell you action must be taken, then direct your managers to do so. Naturally, if the problem is with the managers themselves, you need to fix that situation, pronto.

When you run your property efficiently, you free yourself up to run several of them. That means multiple streams of cash flow, quickly making you a very wealthy investor.

IN THE NEXT CHAPTER

If you've followed my advice so far, you're likely to be owning a great property that's repositioned and streaming cash into your pocket.

But sometimes you'll just want to cash in your chips, and get the big payoff. That's when you must know how to prepare your property to sell for maximum dollars, and that's what the next chapter is all about.

CHAPTER 12

RESELLING FOR HUGE PROFITS

It's harvest time and you've come a very long way. You applied marketing systems to generate leads. You analyzed and bought a property. Then you delegated property management to specialists. You've managed the manager and should be seeing some nice cash flow. Now it's time to sell and get your *big* reward.

You originally bought the property from someone who most likely needed to sell. It might have been due to burnout, or the deferred maintenance/occupancy death spiral. However, you're in a much better position: You could probably hold onto your asset longer, but have decided that the time might be right to cash in your chips.

- Perhaps you see that demographics in your area are starting to change. Maybe your property—once squarely in the path of progress—has started to cool off a bit. The area seems oversupplied, with even more properties slated to be built in the near future. It could be that job growth is slowing in the area, or the current government is not as pro-business as it once was.
- You may have used up most of your depreciation and other tax advantages of owning real estate. Getting into another property would allow you to start getting them all over again.

- Sometimes a partnership dissolves because of the death of one partner or perhaps a divorce. Good partnership agreements spell out exactly what happens when such situations occur.
- You may want to stay in this market, despite noticing a downturn. One excellent strategy is to sell during the strong phase of the cycle, put yourself into a cash position, wait for the full-blown downturn, then scoop up lots of good real estate at bargain prices.
- Or you just might want to act on my favorite reason for selling: To trade up to a bigger property on a tax-deferred basis.

Because you're not buried in day-to-day management of tenants, you can step back and carefully think through your *exit strategy*. If you see one or more good reasons, this could be a great time to sell, especially if the market is still strong.

Here's an example. I found a 32-unit property in an emerging market and bought it for $600,000. It cash-flowed at 11 percent to me after expenses, increasing as the months went by. The market started to appreciate wildly. Within two years, the value had increased to $1,100,000. I sold it and made around $440,000 after expenses.

I then plowed that profit into a 72-unit property, worth $1.6 million, with no money out of my pocket. I now have a larger property in the same market that is still appreciating wildly. In the next 12 months the value should increase by another $500,000, and I'll do it again.

This next time I project to have about $900,000 to invest ($440,000 from the first property profit, and about $500,000 from the second property—give or take).

Let's assume I put 20 percent down on the next property. That means I'll be purchasing a property for $4.5 million. In two hops, I'll have turned a $600,000 property into a $4.5 million one. It will happen with no money out of my pocket. Oh, and a property of that size should send me cash flow of about $10,000 each month. That is why you're still reading this book!

RETURN ON EQUITY

Some investors like to hold their properties forever. They think it's a smart move because they're paying down their mortgages and they like the feeling of owning all their properties *free and clear.*

That's a fine goal if you are not growth-oriented. I personally want to increase my wealth as fast as possible without taking a lot of risk. Owning properties with no debt is not the way to do it.

You must consider your *return on equity*.

First let me warn you: The world of real estate investing has a ton of different calculations you can make. And even the same term, like *return on equity*, has multiple calculations, depending on what you're trying to analyze.

The concept behind return on equity (ROE) is simple: It shows how much you're making on the profits you have to work with. Here's one of the ROE formulas.

It is calculated by dividing the equity you have in your property by the acquisition costs.

$$\text{Return on Equity} = \frac{\text{Cash Flow after Taxes}}{\text{Initial Cash Investment}}$$

So, if your initial equity going into a property was $50,000, and your cash flow was $5,000, then we'd have a 10 percent ROE:

$$\text{Return on Equity of 10\%} = \frac{\text{Cash Flow after Taxes of \$5,000}}{\text{Initial Cash Investment of \$50,000}}$$

That's fine for the first year you own a property. But what if you bought in an appreciating market (as this book is showing you how to do)?

Now, the calculation should be modified to show your *current equity*.

$$\text{Return on Equity} = \frac{\text{Cash Flow after Taxes}}{\text{Current Equity in the Property}}$$

After all, your initial cash investment is most relevant only at the moment you bought the property. While you own it, your equity might shrink to zero if the market tanks, or it may balloon if the market appreciates. The modified equation shown here will tell you how much you're earning on that updated equity number.

Let's say your cash flow is steadily increasing, but appreciation is growing even faster. Now the numbers may look like this:

$$\text{Return on Equity of 8.6\%} = \frac{\text{Cash Flow after Taxes of \$6,000}}{\text{Current Equity of \$70,000}}$$

Look what happened: Everything's working for you in regard to higher cash flow and higher appreciation—but you're losing ground in one sense. That equity is only earning you 8.6 percent now, versus 10 percent earlier. You've got money that is not working as hard as it could for you.

I suggest you take out some of that equity and buy more property. You can do this either by refinancing or selling the property and leveraging up.

To leverage up is to take your profits and turn them into a down payment on a larger property. There is great power in leverage, even though some people are scared of it.

Leverage hurts idiots. If you blindly follow mob emotions and buy when everyone else is, you will buy at the top. If you sell when everyone else is selling—thus giving you that social cushion—then you'll sell at the bottom. Leverage is bad, of course, in that situation. I'd go so far as to say that real estate investing is bad for idiots, but so is the stock market and any other complex investment.

Let's face it: Investing in real estate involves risk. But if you follow basic, tested principles of building your marketing system, buying right, and managing properly, then borrowing money can be a great wealth multiplier.

If you can own three properties with conservative debt on them, versus one property with no debt, you'll make each of your equity dollars benefit you three times as much.

Again, there's nothing wrong with buying with all cash and steadily growing your wealth. I just want you to avoid the black-and-white trap of thinking *debt is bad*. As they say, a knife can either save your life or take it, depending on how it's used. This book and my entire investing approach are all about the sensible, conservative use of every ethical real estate tool to grow wealth quickly.

IS YOUR PROPERTY STABILIZED?

In the process of preparing your property for maximum resale value, the very first thing to do is make sure your property has been *stabilized* for at least three months (six months is ideal). A stabilized property enjoys an occupancy rate of 85 percent or higher.

When you put a stabilized property on the market, you enable buyers to get easier financing. That, in turn, means more potential buyers, which leads to higher prices.

Look at the number of lease-expiration notices your manager will be sending in the next 60 days. Get comfortable that your leasing team will fill *at least* that number of units, but preferably double that number.

There will always be leases that fall through and applicants who never move in. If this happens and your goal was only to cover the expiring leases, you will have a net negative number for future occupancy.

Of course, the other reason to have very active leasing is because the higher your occupancy, the higher your revenues. That results in higher NOI, which leads to a higher sales price.

GET YOUR FINANCIAL HOUSE IN ORDER

As I just said, you increase the value of your property by growing its NOI, or net operating income. We use the *capitalization rate* to determine the property value. (I discussed this in some depth in Chapter 7.)

You affect NOI by increasing revenues and decreasing expenses. On the revenue side, not only should your property be stabilized, but you should try to hit maximum realistic occupancy. It would be a mistake to shoot always for 100 percent occupancy, so that's why I use the word *realistic.*

Wait until you feel you've hit maximum occupancy, and let a couple of months go by so the income is reflected in the profit-and-loss statement. Then put that property on the market.

You can also increase revenues by boosting collections. I spent some time talking about this in the last chapter. One of your jobs in managing your managers is to watch the collection numbers closely. There are always reasons why some rents are still outstanding; on the other hand, I have a property in San Marcos, Texas, where the manager continuously closes her books with 100 percent collections! You can bet we're taking good care of her.

Now look at your expenses. If you're not already running the property very lean, you should start. Don't be so lean that repairs go undone and tenants become dissatisfied! Just make sure there's no fat in the budget.

Each time you have an expense, you must decide how it gets reported in the profit-and-loss statement.

Was it a capital expense or an ordinary expense? *Capital expenses* are bigger repairs that do not come out of normal operating cash. Roof repairs, appliances, carpets, and heating systems are examples of capital items. On the other hand, examples of *ordinary* monthly expenses are repairing fixtures, fixing holes in walls, and painting apartments.

Both types of expenses go onto the profit-and-loss statement, but are handled differently for tax and other purposes.

An ordinary expense results in an immediate, full deduction for tax purposes. A capital expense is considered a longer-term benefit to the property, and gets deducted—or *depreciated*—over time. It can take as long as 27.5 years to deduct that expense fully.

Here is a summary of the profit-and-loss statement:

Income
– Expenses

= NOI
– Debt Service

= Cash Flow before Taxes
– Capital Expenses

= Net Cash Flow

Now you can see why capital expenses can be good, even though it takes longer to deduct them: *Capital expenses don't reduce your NOI, and NOI determines price.*

Use two expense strategies, depending on your investing phase: When you hold property for cash flow and depreciation, it's best to incur as many ordinary expenses as possible. This approach reduces tax liability because you write off or *expense* the cost in the same year it was incurred.

When you are planning to sell a property, it's best to categorize expenses as *capital* whenever possible. They will not reduce your NOI, so your sales price can be higher.

Note that I said to change the expense treatment *whenever possible.* The IRS has rules about what are considered ordinary and capital expenses. Some expenses are borderline, however, and could be categorized either way. Seek the advice of an accountant familiar with real estate and you'll not only save time, but you'll get the best tax treatment for any given expense.

The more lead time you give yourself in planning to sell a property, the better you can position it for resale. I suggest making the decision to sell at least six months in advance, so you can shape up that profit-and-loss statement and squeeze maximum value from your property.

GET YOUR PHYSICAL HOUSE IN ORDER

Now that you're planning ahead and getting your P&L in order, it's also time to review the physical aspect of your property. You want it to look *really good.*

Of course, you should have a maintenance program that keeps your property looking good at all times. But if there's ever a time to make it absolutely shine, this is it. The side benefit is that a super-well-maintained property will be that much easier to lease up, at the best rates.

Many shortsighted landlords make the mistake of skimping on repairs so they can keep more cash in their pockets. As I discussed earlier, this just makes the repairs more expensive later on. And buyers will factor those more expensive repairs into their offers to buy the property.

So check out that property and make sure everything is in tip-top shape. Here are some of the key items you should focus on:

- Is all interior and exterior paint in good shape?
- Is the siding intact, or are there problem areas needing repair?
- Is all woodwork solid throughout the property?
- Does the roof need to be repaired or replaced?
- Can the landscaping be upgraded or trimmed back?
- Is the parking lot in good shape?

- Is the laundry room neat, clean, and in 100 percent working order?
- Are all windows and screens intact with zero cracks or holes?
- Are all doors on apartments the same color and looking good?
- Is every light working outside, and is the exterior lighting on photo (light-sensitive) cells?
- Is the mailbox area neat and clean, and are all the mail boxes the same?
- Are the common area hallways looking good? Do they need paint, carpet, or lighting?
- Is the basement clean and not a dumping ground for forgotten storage items?
- Is all fencing and metalwork in good shape outside?
- Are there any electrical issues?
- Are there any plumbing issues?
- Is the septic tank working properly?
- Are balconies in good shape?
- Is the pool area neat, clean, and inviting, with clear water in the pool?
- If you have a leasing office, is it in good shape, with furniture that is not worn out?
- If you have a maintenance shed, is it organized, neat, and clean?

You get the idea. Walk your property and look at everything that might give buyers an excuse to offer a lower price. Then make those excuses disappear.

TIME TO TELL THE WORLD

Now that both your financial and physical house is in order, it's time to tell the world you're ready to sell. You can do this by either selling the property yourself, or using a broker to list it.

My rule of thumb: If a broker sold me the deal, that broker now gets the listing. That way, she will continue to give me more deals. I'm definitely on her A list. If you do *not* use the same broker, word will get around. It's like slapping her in the face and telling her to get out of your life.

Some investors make the mistake of selling it themselves so they can save on commissions.

You'll save money on commissions, all right. But are you in this business for the long term? If so, your few bucks of savings just cost you the opportunity to see more and better deals.

There's another reason to use brokers: The ability to close the deal is key. Someone can make a great offer for your property, but if the buyer cannot or does not close, it's worthless to you. When you sell the property yourself, you almost never have a prior relationship with the buyer.

Brokers make it their business to know the best sellers and the best buyers of property. They earn that commission by making the sales process easier on you.

Here's something to watch out for, though: Brokers can sometimes have a property sold before it even hits the market. Now, *when we are buyers of properties*, we want to get the listing and put a property under contract before it hits the market. That reduces competition and we might get a lower price. When we're selling, we want the opposite: We want competition.

The Call to Offer

Good brokers will do this by preparing a *call to offer*. They will create a property package and send it to their entire list. Some offices work together and send it to everyone's list in that office.

The property package tells everything buyers need to know about the property, including *pro forma* financials. It also includes a deadline date for all offers.

By not putting a price on the property, brokers are asking for the highest bid. They are truly letting the market set the price. As a buyer, I don't like bidding on these properties and very seldom win. If there's a deal I really like, I will offer, call the broker, let him know that I know that I probably won't be the highest price—but want to be considered a backup offer.

This approach sometimes works. The top bidder might state a great price, but can't get financing. At this point, the seller is not only disappointed, but wants to make *sure* the next one goes through. This is when the broker will recommend a buyer with a proven performance record—that should be you.

Back to the *call to offer*: As a seller, I like for the broker to go through this process. It's usually when I get my highest price. After the initial deadline passes, the broker will take the top five offers and ask for *best and final.* Then bidders give their best-and-final offer. The broker then asks for the *final offer.* Crazy, isn't it! But that's how it's done, and it usually results in the highest price.

Let's say I bought the property directly from an owner, or maybe from a broker with whom I have no interest in working. I'll then either offer it to the next most valuable broker—someone who has given me other business, or a broker I want to cultivate.

If no broker comes to mind, I might attempt to sell it myself. First I go to loopnet.com and list the property.

As I mentioned before, Loopnet is a nationwide and worldwide source for listing commercial real estate. You can list any property on loopnet.com for free. You don't have to be a broker or hold any licenses. You'll get exposure to all kinds of buyers: Some are serious, many are tire-kickers, and a few are whackos.

If people respond to your listing, ask them two key questions:

1. How many units do you own?
2. Are you willing to provide me with proof of funds?

The answer to Question 1 will tell you how long they've been playing the game, and whether they are a performer. Trust me: The *wannabes* will sound incredibly energetic and even highly confident; but it's results that count. Choose the strongest buyer for your property.

If they're okay with Question 2 and are willing to show you proof of funds, you've got one or more strong buyers. If they are not willing to show you proof of funds, *go to the next buyer.* They are not going to close on the deal, no matter how much they offered you!

Now get the name and number of the buyer's lender so you can track the progress. You'll need to get written permission from the buyer to do this, or the lender will not talk with you.

You must track the progress because last-minute wrenches have a way of materializing and throwing themselves into the machinery. With early warning, sometimes you can prevent that from happening. Other times, at least your early warning will give you longer to find another buyer.

YOUR OBLIGATIONS AS A SELLER

You will typically have 14 days after you sign the *purchase-and-sale agreement* to forward the financial due diligence package to the buyer.

As you know, the sales price is based on net operating income. You stated what that NOI was during the offer process—now it's time for you to prove it.

Here's what you'll forward:

- Last two years' profit-and-loss statements
- Year-to-date and monthly operating statements
- Current rent roll
- Current mortgage note
- A copy of the survey

Because you're a smart seller, you've been preparing for this phase for at least six months, remember? Therefore, it's not a mad scramble to collect the materials. You've calmly been putting your due diligence package together for a while now. When the buyer requests the package, you'll make a great impression by blasting it right over by overnight delivery.

I don't need to explain the steps that will happen from this point on, because I already described them in earlier chapters (in the context of when you buy a property).

Yes, you've put a lot of time in on this property over the last months or years (though not as a landlord!). You've even received some good cash flow up to this point. Now you will reap a very substantial harvest: All your *managing of the managers* is paying off, in the form of a cashier's check with lots of zeros!

IN THE NEXT CHAPTER

Sometimes your success will be measured not just by how many things you do right, but also by how many mistakes you avoid.

I've already told you about many blunders inexperienced investors make. I discuss next the biggies that can bring down your investing career in a hurry.

CHAPTER 13

The 10 Biggest Mistakes Repositioners Make, and How to Avoid Them

Don't believe the hucksters who talk about real estate investing like it's an absolute *sure thing*. I have some bad news and good news for you. First, the bad:

Real estate involves risk. If people are looking for an excellent risk-free return that will make them financially set for life, they're just dumber than a bag of hammers.

The good news: A few real estate investors—like you—actually get off their duffs and acquire knowledge. When that knowledge is from someone who's been highly successful, the odds of success suddenly get far better.

Here are 10 mistakes, in no particular order. I've referred to a few of them already, but really want to drive them home now. I envy the opportunity before you! By simply reading and following my advice, you can save yourself literally years of trouble and up to millions of dollars in lost profit. What I wouldn't have given for this advice when I started out!

Mistake #1: Running Out of Money During a Repositioning

This is truly a *lose-lose situation*, and one of the biggest mistakes you can make. You can end up getting 95 percent of the way to the goal (making big money), and be stopped dead in your tracks. Even worse, you then forfeit your property to someone who reaps those rewards with 5 percent of the effort.

Repositioners run out of money because of cost overruns and time delays. You must put a *no overage* clause in all of your contracts with contractors.

Here's an overage: A contractor says: "Mr. Lindahl, we've got a problem. That roof you contracted us to do for $40,000? Well, it will be $50,000 because. . . ."

You must tell the contractor *up front* that you do not allow overages and he must anticipate any problems that might happen during the repair process. You're happy to discuss those problems *before* the job starts. You will get much better prices if you price out anticipated problems before the job starts, versus when the contractor is already on the job.

Let's say you ask a roofer to do your roofs and his price is $40,000. You then ask: "Mr. Roofer, what would happen if you strip off those shingles and find rotted sheathing below? How much would you charge me per sheet of sheathing replacement?"

He then gives you a price, so you know what it will cost to replace that sheathing *if* it's later found to be rotted.

If you fail to do this, you've just entered the contractor's biggest profit zone.

Simply walk the property with each contractor ahead of time. It's not your job to know everything that can go wrong with the job. The contractor already knows this. It's your job to make sure the contractors anticipate problems and give you the potential costs.

If a contractor will not agree to this approach, get another contractor. It's nonnegotiable.

Here is another critical point: When there actually is an overage, the contractor *must not* simply start doing the work. Your contract must state that the contractor is required to notify you of the overage before addressing it. You then come out and inspect the proposed extra work. You then finalize the price that was negotiated earlier, and you both sign the overage form.

Only when you have both signed the overage form will the contractor get paid for the overage. You must spell that out specifically in your contract, and you should *discuss it* with the contractor ahead of time. Contractors love to bid a job low, knowing they will make it up on the overages.

I repositioned a 192-unit property in Arlington, Texas. I decided that the leasing office was too far back on the property and wanted to move it closer to the entry gate.

We had to take down a couple of walls because we were combining a storage unit and two one-bedroom units to make up the new office. We got several complete bids and chose the lowest bid from a contractor with whom we had done business in the past.

The city decided that the amount of repairs we were doing was enough to trigger the Americans with Disabilities Act (ADA). That meant the new leasing office had to be handicapped-accessible throughout.

The contractor must have been jumping for joy! We had not anticipated this and now he had a big change order on his hands. All the walls were already down, the fixtures had been stripped, the materials were on site, and the contractor was firmly entrenched in the job. The change order was in excess of $42,000, and I had no choice. That was a $42,000 lesson for Old Dave.

I pay attention when I have $42,000 lessons. Some time later, I bought another property, this time with 356 units. The night before the seller was supposed to sign the purchase-and-sale agreement, the leasing office burned down. Eighty percent destroyed. What a great negotiating position we were in!

The contractors had already bid the job, but we now had to add rebuilding of the leasing office. We got the bids in and—surprise!—not one single contractor mentioned even the possibility of the ADA coming into play.

Having learned my lesson, I knew it would have to conform, and so did they. We required that the contractor be responsible for building a structure that conformed to ADA standards. Did they ever scramble to change their bids!

Of course, you reduce your risk even further by asking around for reputable contractors, and getting several bids for each job.

As I mentioned in an earlier chapter, you can come in on or under budget, but late. That's also bad.

If your contractor takes longer than anticipated, you will not have revenues from units you thought would be leased up by a certain date. This is why it's so important for your construction manager to keep that contractor on site and on schedule. Time delays can ruin you.

Then make sure the leasing agents are doing their job. It's important that they lease up that property fast. We already discussed the critical importance of a comprehensive marketing plan, together with reports that tell you traffic, new applicants, approved tenants, and so on.

Time really is money in the multi-family business.

MISTAKE #2: LEASING UP TOO SOON

That sounds strange, doesn't it? I just told you one of the ways you will run out of money is by not leasing up quickly. Now am I telling you the opposite?

No, says Goldilocks. You want the lease-up to happen at the *just right* speed. The success of your repositioning project depends in part on changing perceptions, then changing your tenant base.

First comes the new image of the property. The community has a low opinion of your property right now; that's why you bought it, complete with some undesirable tenants. Tenants matching your target profile most likely share that low opinion of your property. Only when they judge that the riff-raff has moved on will the new tenants move in.

I discussed at some length earlier about the process you'll take to change the community's opinion of your property. Word of mouth takes time. If you start marketing too soon, the only people moving in will be the type you just kicked out. They'll not appreciate your improvements, and they will soon drag down the property to its pre-repositioning condition.

Let me put it to you more bluntly: Even if you do a perfect physical repositioning, it won't help, because you're trying to rush the *psychological* repositioning.

How do you know when perceptions have changed? Even before you roll out your full marketing plan, you'll be getting traffic from walk-ins, and some of them will be your target profile. The first great sign will be when you're able to charge higher rents to that better tenant class.

Great sign number two: When those tenants start to refer the property to their friends and co-workers, who begin to move in. It's *then* that you roll out your full-blown marketing.

I've got a 396-unit property in Alabama. We bought it at *40 percent occupancy*. That's over 230 vacant units! It was a wild place with a bad reputation.

I remember having dinner at the bar of a popular fish chain. The bartender asked me what I was doing there; I guess my accent gave away that I didn't grow up in the South.

I told her that I buy and sell apartments and I was visiting my property. "Oh yeah, which one?" I mentioned it by its previous name because our new name was too new. Her reaction: "Do you carry a gun?"

Only nine months later, we hit 82 percent occupancy and kept climbing. Our biggest source of traffic and lease-up was tenant referrals. The perception had changed!

MISTAKE #3: NOT USING LICENSED CONTRACTORS

Everyone's looking to save money. You definitely should watch expenses very carefully. Nevertheless, the one place *not* to skimp on is hiring quality workers.

There are times when you can get away with using handymen. As the term implies, they're good for small jobs like replacing appliances, doing light carpentry work, replacing broken trim, and tasks of similar magnitude.

When you must pull a permit to get a job done, hire only licensed workers. How do you know when you'll need a permit pulled? Your local building, wiring, and plumbing inspectors will be able to give you a list of jobs that require permits. When in doubt as to whether you need a permit, call the local inspectors and they will tell you.

Even if a handyman says he can handle one of these permit-pulling jobs, don't allow him to. In most cases, you'll be left with a job that wasn't done properly; you'll have to get it repaired; and now you're on the bad side of the inspectors! (More on that in a minute.) Besides, licensed contractors usually have both liability insurance and workers' comp insurance. That coverage is rare with handymen.

I've been doing rehabs and repositioning projects for the last 14 years. Here's the difference between handymen and licensed contractors: Full-time handymen never got their business act together. They live from job to job, never taking the time to build systems to get them to the level of a bona fide business. You should instead be dealing with professionals for the big jobs.

Handymen can't pull permits because they aren't licensed. You must make sure you get permits on jobs that require them! If you get caught doing a job that requires a permit and you didn't pull one, you'll have a bright orange *stop-work order* plastered on your front door.

After you finally do what you should have done in the first place and pull the permit, the inspector will come out and do the first inspection. Knowing that you tried to get away with something, do you think the inspector will be tough or easy on you? And do you think it will end with that job? Absolutely not. You'll now have a reputation as a troublemaker. It could take years to make these people relax and finally treat you pleasantly.

MISTAKE #4: NOT GETTING THREE BIDS

Definitely get a minimum of three bids. Many investors skip this step because they didn't start the bidding process until after they closed on the property. Now they're having problems locating contractors and getting them out to their site. Then even more time passes before they actually get bids. They're so grateful finally to get one contractor to bid that they go with that person.

This is an easily avoided mistake. When you sign the purchase-and-sale agreement with the seller, get permission to allow your contractors on site for inspections and bidding.

While you're doing your due diligence, you will also be preparing to get the project started as soon as you close. During the due diligence phase, get those three or more contractors on site (not all at the same time) and have them give you bids.

Let them know when you expect them to start, which will be on or near the closing date. Knowing the start date will motivate them to give you the bids.

What if you get only two bids to come in before the closing? At least you have two bids and not just one, and you're not in panic mode to get the job done.

MISTAKE #5: ASSUMING THE LOWEST BID IS THE BEST BID

It's a mistaken temptation to think that whoever comes in lowest should get the job.

As I said earlier, some contractors make a living by *low-balling* their bids, then finding ways to get more money from you while the work is in progress.

The low bid is sometimes the best one, but only sometimes. You can protect yourself from low-balling contractors by giving all bidders a spec sheet on which they will be bidding. That sheet gives the specific bidding instructions for each job, so they're all bidding on the same items.

Require your contractors to list all tasks they will perform, and give you separate costs. Do not accept a general description of what will be done and only a lump-sum cost.

You might wonder why I have them list everything if I've already given them a spec sheet. Even though you gave them the sheet, if they don't list everything again on their bid, it's one of the ways they try to come back later and stick you for an overage.

Also, if you want to subtract anything from the job while it's in progress, you will know how much to take off the total bill.

Whenever you get a bid that seems to be much lower than all the others, review it item-by-item with the contractor before accepting, and compare it to all your requirements for the job. Sometimes, they simply didn't understand the bid and will tell you so when you perform this joint review.

Be a tough negotiator, but up to a point: Although you should get the job done for a great price, the contractor must not only cover his costs but make a decent profit. Yet some contractors will bid a job below this reasonable-cost-and-profit figure. Maybe they're desperate for work, or bad at estimating.

If you accept such a bid—thinking you're a world-class negotiator—you may be in for trouble. At some point, the contractor will realize he can't do the job for what he bid. He'll either ask you for more money or will walk off the job. To avoid embarrassment, they usually walk off the job without telling you. Then you'll waste a great deal of time chasing them down and browbeating them to get back on site.

When you get three bids from a contractor, always trust your gut. This is the best advice I can give you. You have three people, one of whom you are about to marry for the next several months or years. If your gut tells you this is not the right person, don't hire him! No matter how low his bid is, don't hire him. Trust me on this.

MISTAKE #6: NOT GOING AFTER PRIVATE MONEY SOONER

People naturally avoid lining up financing when they don't know how. It doesn't matter if you're a big or small investor: You need private money to grow your business. The sooner you get your sources in place, the faster your business will grow.

I devoted an entire chapter on *private money* and how to attract it. It is one of the Big Three Action Steps you must continuously take to make your business thrive (marketing and continuing your education are the other two).

Private money is the key to the growth vault. The best part about private money is that there are so many starving people, so to speak, willing to lend you money to invest because they want better returns.

Once you perform as you said you would, your investors will start to brag about the great return they're getting from doing business with you. They become your sales force and will bring you even more private money.

I had an investor who invested $100,000 in one of my deals. Investors were projected to get a 9 percent cash return the first year, and the overall annualized return was projected at 24 percent (after the deal was eventually sold).

When we consistently returned over 10 percent, the investor began telling his friends, who have now invested just under $1 million. Now those friends are happy, and word-of-mouth is spreading.

The best private money marketing you can do is by word-of-mouth referral, but there are certain proven principles here, too. If you want to get comfortable with methods beyond the scope of this book, I conduct a live event devoted to the topic. For more information, just go to MultiFamilyMillions.com and enter the keywords *private money*.

Once you have your stable of investors, you'll very quickly see your business explode. Think of the confidence you will display when you're out negotiating deals, knowing that you have all the money you need to take those deals down!

MISTAKE #7: NOT MARKETING CONSISTENTLY

Marketing is the engine that ultimately moves your business toward your goals.

You'll need to market for both deals and private money. Many investors do a little marketing for deals and are delighted when it works. They get a deal or two under contract, and then focus all their time on getting the deals done.

You must walk and chew gum at the same time. You must get those deals done, but also continue your marketing. If you don't, your business will go *from feast to famine*: The feast occurs after you close your deal and get rewarded with cash flow and maybe a big check.

But if you haven't been consistently marketing, you'll soon realize there's nothing in your pipeline. You will be in famine mode until that next deal arrives.

Again, if you want to take a casual stroll toward wealth, then by all means turn your marketing on and off. If you want get to your financial goals fast, you must market continuously.

MISTAKE #8: DISCRIMINATING

If you or anyone in your organization gets caught discriminating, you risk being slapped with fines of more than $10,000.

That's right, I said *you or anyone in your organization.* If someone else discriminates and gets caught, the hammer will fall on you. That's why you must educate your employees about discrimination and how to avoid it.

As I briefly mentioned in another chapter, the government has *testers*. These people will call or visit your office and pretend they want to rent an apartment. They'll ask you typical questions on the phone and they may ask to see the property.

The very next day—or very next hour—another person will call or visit and will follow the same general routine, but will be a different race. If you don't treat that person identically, you've discriminated.

The government says that you cannot discriminate based on race, color, national origin, religion, sex, familial status, or handicap.

Here's a short list of what you cannot do, based on color, race, and so on:

Refuse to rent housing.

Provide different housing services or facilities.

Falsely deny that housing is available for rental.

I suggest you get familiar with the Housing and Urban Development site at www.hud.gov and look up the *Fair Housing Act*. That site has good training materials for you and your staff. Discrimination is a very large potential minefield, yet it's so easy to avoid.

MISTAKE #9: NOT HAVING SIGNING AUTHORITY ON BANK ACCOUNTS

I covered this one in an earlier chapter, but it still is one of the biggest mistakes you can make. You absolutely must have signing authority on bank accounts, or your manager may hold those funds hostage if any disagreements arise.

You can be dead right in regard to the facts—but you'll be dead all the same if you cannot access the bank accounts of your property in a timely fashion.

As I told you earlier, some management companies will state: "It's our policy to be the sole authorized signers because we've been harmed by owners who drain the accounts and left us to pay the bills."

You then say: "Well, it's my policy to work only with management companies that are okay with the owner's having access to the owner's own funds."

If they stand their ground, move on to the next management company. There may be an underlying reason they don't want to give up control, and it can't be good.

MISTAKE #10: BUYING A PROPERTY WITH ENVIRONMENTAL ISSUES

You must get familiar with what's called an *Environmental Phase One Report*. It will tell you about any known or suspected contaminants on the site.

Make *sure* you have a Phase One done on the property. It's usually required by lenders on properties larger than six units. Even if you're buying a smaller property, it's smart to get the report done. The couple of thousand dollars is cheap insurance.

A certified company will inspect the soil, water, siding, basement, and paint. It will also do an overall visual inspection, looking for problems.

What problems? Asbestos, radon gas, oil contaminants, run-off contamination from your neighbors' property, pollutants in the water, mold—anything that would affect the health of the people living at the property. These problems also directly affect your ability to resell that property.

The Phase One is the first step. If the property is clean, you're done. If the property has a problem, you go into *Phase Two*. This phase costs a lot more—think tens of thousands of dollars.

One of my students recently called me for advice. She's thinking of buying a 256-unit property in Houston, Texas. A dry cleaner used to be located across the street and contamination had leaked into the ground on one very small corner of the apartment complex.

The contamination was 28 feet below ground and inspectors determined it would slowly dissipate over the years. Her lender required her to take out an insurance policy for which the *premium* cost $100,000. She negotiated with the buyer to split that cost, and wanted my opinion of the deal.

I told her that I would walk away. The pollutants may or may not follow the experts' predictions; but I was more concerned that she'd have a very difficult time reselling the property.

After all, future lenders may have a different attitude about the contamination. If no buyer can get financing, she will not be able to sell it at all, much less at a profit.

Be very concerned about who are—or were—your potential neighbors. Gas stations make for bad neighbors, as do storage facilities (even *they* sometimes don't know what people are storing there).

There are too many good deals out there to complicate your life with properties compromised by environmental issues. Down the road when you get extremely comfortable with evaluating properties, you can consider taking on such a challenge—if the rewards are spectacular compared to the risk. Otherwise, don't bother.

I like to under-promise and over-deliver. In that spirit, here are a few more mistakes you can easily avoid if you're aware of them:

MISTAKE #11: INSPECTING THE PROPERTY YOURSELF

I've been playing this game for 14 years. I started out knowing nothing about real estate, but worked hard to soak up information wherever I could find it: I went to Home Depot night classes, helped out on construction crews, and talked with countless investors.

I've done hundreds of rehabs, either for my own portfolio or for lending institutions. I also became a licensed general contractor. At the risk of sounding immodest, I really am very good at judging properties, what's wrong with them, and how they can be fixed.

What's my point? *I still don't do my own property inspections.*

I always want someone coming in behind me to say: "Hey Dave, you were right about this," or: "Hey Dave, look what you missed. . . ."

It's the *you missed* part I really want to hear. As buyers, we are far too busy to be going through a property meticulously. You and I are also not experienced in the ins and outs of countless types of heating and cooling systems, structural combinations, and building codes. While you keep your eye on the big picture, you must delegate this specialty to the specialists.

On smaller multi-family properties, a regular home inspector is fine.

For larger properties, you need a licensed property inspector or civil engineer with specific experience inspecting multi-family properties. The inspector will review all mechanical and structural components, and will go into some (not all) of the units. It is *your job* to inspect every single unit, as I mentioned in an earlier chapter.

Major systems are the main focus of the inspector: roof, structural components, boilers, cooling, and so on—things that cost lots of money to fix.

MISTAKE #12: MANAGING THE PROPERTY YOURSELF

I know I'm a broken record on this point, but I'm on a mission: I want you *not* to save a few bucks on property management, and end up so burned out that you dump real estate investing altogether.

That's exactly what will happen if you try to manage a property yourself.

Did you get interested in real estate as a way to free yourself, or just add more burdens and headaches to your life? In my opinion, you're better off not doing real estate at all rather than become a 24-hour handyman for tenants.

From Day One you can avoid that misery by creating an effective marketing machine that brings you a steady stream of leads. Then focus only on properties that can support a property manager.

On the smaller properties it will cost you more, and you'll only get a part-time person. That's okay, because *you* are not that person! Larger properties can support a full-time manager for less cost. Either way, the numbers must support property management, or else don't do the deal.

MISTAKE #13: USING FILL-IN-THE-BLANK LEGAL FORMS

I'm a big fan of smart shortcuts in real estate. Using fill-in-the-blank forms is a dumb shortcut.

You must get an attorney—licensed in the state you're investing in—to read through all your paperwork. That goes for documents as standard as the *purchase-and-sale agreement*, or *P & S*. You have no idea what each state requires, and several states have that adolescent habit of just *wanting to be different,* for no good reason. If you're not careful, a local attorney for the seller just might slip a few things into the P & S to make that document biased in favor of the seller.

Hey, that's their job! I don't hold it against them; I just want to be the one with the smarter attorney. With your attorney's help, you can have that extra advantage, or at least have a balanced document.

Your attorney will also help you with many other aspects of the due diligence process. I discuss more about that in the next chapter.

The good ones are worth every penny. To find that gem, make sure you work your referral network of brokers, other investors, property managers, lenders, and anyone else who might know a good attorney.

I also see investors trying to save a buck by filling in the blanks of partnership agreements and other paperwork required by the Securities and Exchange Commission. If you do this, you are just plain crazy. Get that first draft from wherever you can, but definitely run it all by a securities attorney before using any of it.

By the way, attorneys are like doctors: You wouldn't have a foot doctor operate on your brain. Therefore, you shouldn't have a family attorney try to become an expert in multi-family real estate, or securities. They're different disciplines. Maybe you'll find one attorney who can do it all, but that's rare. You must require the attorney to have substantial experience in these areas.

This advice will cost you more money up front, and save you far more down the road.

MISTAKE #14: DEALING WITH TENANTS

This point is different from the one we already covered in *Mistake 12.* There are many owners who hire property managers, yet still get involved with tenants.

They get sucked into tenant disputes, collecting rents, and other issues. You want to be *aware* of these issues, but not involved with tenants.

The management company must keep you informed of issues and ask your opinion when important decisions must be made. Do not train your tenants to think you're available to get involved! Likewise, do not allow your manager to *delegate upward* and have you resolve an issue that he or she should be handling.

Never answer a phone call from a tenant! If you do, it will be the beginning of the end for you. Please understand: I'm not advocating that you ignore problems or disrespect your tenants. On the contrary, you should have determined by now that I advocate excellent tenant relations—*between the tenants and the manager.*

Here's one exception to the rule I just laid down: If a tenant somehow finds my phone number and leaves a message on my voice mail to the effect that something very bad is going on at the property, perhaps involving the manager, I'll use my judgment. If I'm told there is an abusive or discriminating manager, I'd naturally call the tenant back and find out what's going on.

That might happen to you once or twice in your career, but don't let that situation suck you into taking tenant calls regularly.

MISTAKE #15: THINKING YOU KNOW IT ALL

I remember when I was three years into this business. I had accumulated 104 units, and had well over $10,000 a month streaming into my house. I had gone from flat broke to multi-millionaire in three years.

I remember sitting at my desk one day, thinking: *I'm all set. I don't have to read another book, listen to another audiotape, or go to another seminar—ever. I've got it all!*

Boy, was I wrong.

I decided to go to just one more seminar because the topic interested me. After sitting through it, I discovered a technique that increased my income during the next year by almost 25 percent! If I hadn't gone to that seminar, I wouldn't have discovered the technique.

I realized that if I didn't keep acquiring knowledge, I might miss out on many more techniques I could use to make more money. I also realized that by working with other people, I could grow my business even faster and create much more wealth for my family and myself.

Looking back, I'm proud of what I accomplished in just three years, but I also shake my head at the whole world of systems and techniques I had no clue about at the time. So I'm also proud that I didn't just settle back on the couch and stagnate.

The world of business and real estate changes and reinvents itself regularly. Many principles remain the same, but technology and smart people are continuously creating new opportunities. The more you and I stay plugged into this continuing education, the more money we'll make. It's as simple as that.

It seems one thing all successful people have in common is that they never stop discovering. Think about that and take action.

IN THE NEXT CHAPTER

As you know, *leverage* means using the small end of something to create big effects. So far I've talked a lot about leverage. For instance:

- Using little or none of your own money to buy big properties
- Making relatively small improvements that result in large profits

Well, there's another extremely powerful form of leverage—it's the team you'll build to get you to your goals far faster than if you plodded along by yourself. Meet your team in the next chapter.

CHAPTER 14

CREATING YOUR SUCCESS TEAM

I know some *rugged individualists*, but none of them is a rich real estate investor.

If you simply must do it all yourself, real estate is not for you. Maybe take up stock trading in front of the computer. The wealthiest real estate investors realize it's a team effort, and they build a great one. Each person on that team is a specialist who fills an important function.

Remember that I started out with less than $800 to my name. So I know what you're thinking: *Dave, I can't afford a team. I can't even afford myself.*

Believe me, I understand. But I also know that if you've read all the way up to where you are now—Chapter 14—it means you want to break into multi-family investing and get wealthy quickly. I'm pointing out the way.

You don't need all these team members up front. But the sooner you get people to help you, the more quickly you'll get rich. Brian Tracy, the superb business coach and philosopher, has an excellent perspective on this: He says that becoming successful is not like a sit-down dinner at a restaurant, where you get to eat before you pay. Tracy says success is more like a cafeteria, where you pick what you want, but you must pay before you sit down to eat.

Find ways to begin to assemble this team. They will make you embarrassingly rich.

The key players on your power team are:

- Real estate brokers
- Property manager
- Attorneys
- Property inspector
- Appraisers
- Lender
- Contractors
- Insurance agent
- Demographer
- 1031 specialists
- Accountant

REAL ESTATE BROKERS

I listed these specialists in the order they usually come into your life. Note that real estate brokers are the first people on the list. Without deal flow, you don't even have a glimmer of a business. Brokers are the shortest route to being fed deals on a regular basis.

We already talked at some length about how to cultivate brokers. I want to elaborate here on the two kinds of brokers you'll run across.

The *not-so-good brokers* will send you deals with *pro forma* numbers that are way out of line. Remember, *pro forma* numbers do not yet exist, but are projections of what could happen if the planets align themselves just so.

You may find these brokers easier to cultivate, because they'd be just tickled pink to have you buy one of these deals. They know the property does not generate the cash flow it should; but they're romancing you on the deal to get the highest price for their client (and the most commission for themselves).

Imagine buying a business where the owner says: "So my sales this year were not great. But wait until next year! If you buy this business, it's on a fast track to do way better next year! Oh, by the way, I think I'm entitled to some of those profits next year, so I'll just base my sales price for the business on next year's projections—okay?"

After you finished laughing, you'd tell him to go jump in a lake. Believe it or not, this is done in real estate all the time by certain brokers—and you should have the same response.

The *good brokers* recognize that all purchases of multi-family properties should be based on actual numbers, because that's how lenders finance them. These brokers also realize you'll look at certain ratios and need a competitive return on your money, not only to stay in business but also to get bank financing.

Far-sighted brokers want long-term relationships with investors. They know those relationships can be worth tens or *hundreds* of thousands of dollars in commissions.

Good brokers price their listings fairly and want to work with good investors. Those investors run their properties profitably and turn back to the brokers to sell them. Everyone wins.

Get as many good brokers in your stable as you possibly can. Remember my three cardinal rules for standing out from the investor crowd:

1. Make it easy to do business with you
2. Do what you say you will do
3. Don't be a pain in the butt

Many brokers cooperate with each other more than they compete. If you build good relationships with a few brokers, pretty soon they'll refer you to other brokers, and will be happy to give you a good reference, too.

THE PROPERTY MANAGER

After you get a property under contract, it's time to start talking with property managers. If you don't know many players in a given market, it makes sense to contact property managers even before you get a property under contract. That way you can ask them to refer you to some good brokers.

If the managers have been in the market for any length of time, they know the good, bad, and ugly brokers. It's in the managers' best interest to help you out, because they hope you'll remember them when you buy a property.

Make sure that you get the best manager you can find, who also specializes in your specific type of property.

This team member is crucial because once you have a property under contract, the management company will help you perform due diligence. This is especially valuable when you're buying property in an emerging market that's far from home.

You can ask that management company to drive to the property and look for any major defects. They'll report on the condition of the roof, siding, landscaping, and many other exterior aspects, just from driving past the site.

Though the seller will give you property pictures, you might not know how old those pictures are, or whether they've been retouched so they're not really representative of the property. Pictures from your property manager will be more objective.

Your manager might even *shop* the property (that is, pretend to be a potential tenant). Now you'll have solid, current information on what some of the insides look like, too.

Think of the time you save when the manager gives you this information before you come out to the property. If the property's really bad, you'll know it without having blown much time at all. If it's only partly bad—for instance, the roofs need replacing and you weren't told that by the seller—you can start negotiating those roofs even before you get there.

If the seller decides not to negotiate the roofs, you've just saved yourself time, money, and disappointment. Be sure to reward this manager for saving you a lot of time and effort, even if a deal falls through. A big box of gourmet cookies will work.

I hope you see how a strong relationship with property managers can be so incredibly beneficial. Compare that to amateur investors, who get excited about a property and schedule a visit as the first task. You can just sit back and smile—they won't be in business for long.

Note: Do *not* send the manager over until *after* you have the property under agreement. If you can, don't read ahead but just tell me why I would say such a thing.

Here's why: If you send the manager over before you have the contract signed, you run the risk of the management company buying the property out from under you! Or they might call an investor pal and have that person put in a bid, knowing they will definitely get the management contract.

The management company will also help you to create a budget, marketing plan, and five-year *pro forma*. You want to see all this information yourself, and the lender will want to see it in the loan package.

It's possible that you'll have multiple management companies in the same market, because most firms specialize in a few property types. If a company tells you it can manage anything, just ask for a list of its current portfolio of properties. You should quickly detect what type of property receives the most attention.

ATTORNEYS

First, you put a property under contract with a letter of intent or offer; then you sign a purchase-and-sale agreement. The seller usually provides the P & S.

As I mentioned in the last chapter, it's a big mistake to try to save a few bucks at this stage. P & S agreements look official, but are subject to lots of tweaks by lawyers. I guess if both you and the seller are cheap, then you might luck out with a fairly neutral P & S. Don't take that chance.

Get professional advice from an *experienced real estate attorney* before you start to sign things. You can usually get referrals from brokers in the area. They know who the good ones are because they have to deal with them each time a property is sold. You can also get referrals from the local landlord association or real estate investment group.

Your network can help you in the other direction, too. Once you have a good attorney, you can ask for referrals to good brokers and property managers. It's all about your network.

I had to ask around, but then I got lucky: Someone told me about Robert Reed, an attorney in Brockton, Massachusetts. Here are the qualifications you want in an attorney:

- Been in business for years
- Specializes in real estate
- Looks out for his clients' best interest
- Vast knowledge
- Is willing to get creative, but also recognizes the boundaries of the law when things get too creative
- Easy to get along with (where did we hear that before?)

Bob Reed is all that and more. I remember closing my first deal with Bob. He took a look at the trust I was using and asked: "Who did this trust?"

I proudly told him I went to a class that a local real estate guru held on how to create your own trusts. This was the trust the guru gave us to use. The guru said it was absolutely *bullet-proof.* Eleven pages of hardened armor.

Bob sighed. Then in a patient tone he proceeded to tell me how this trust was a piece of &*$% and pointed out how it exposed me in no fewer than five areas! He was so concerned that I would go down in flames on my first deal that he *gave me* his own trust to use. He didn't even know me, and could have charged me a bundle for the trust document. But already he was looking out for me. It's a document I still use today when I'm flipping smaller properties. How many attorneys do you know who would freely hand you anything other than a bill? (Thanks, Bob!)

A good real estate attorney can also sometimes get a tax assessment lowered. I have an attorney who practices in one of the emerging markets I invest in. I paid her $7,000 to try to get our tax assessment lower. She did, to the tune of a $56,000 tax reduction.

You also will eventually need a litigation attorney on your team. Sooner or later, you will either sue someone or get sued. It's just a matter of time, and it's not unique to real estate investing. Don't get all nervous on me: It's just part of doing business.

I'm not even thinking of tenants right now. Sure, they will sue you, too, but your insurance will take care of them. Insurance companies typically settle out of court for a predetermined amount, regardless of whether the tenant is right or wrong.

I know that sounds strange, but it's true. On two occasions I got sued and I *knew* the incident did not happen on my property. The insurance company didn't care. It just settled. Sometimes it's cheaper to settle than to go to court and prove innocence. On other occasions, I've gone after tenants who filed frivolous suits and they ended up not only dropping the suit, but paying me damages.

No, it's not the tenants, but other parties in a transaction: Either they will sue you or it will be the other way around.

You want a kick-butt litigation attorney who is as vicious as a dog who's been tied on a rope and hasn't eaten for a week. It's the person in town that no one wants to be in court against. You can find this SOB by asking your brokers, managers, and other members on your team. Experienced people in town know who this person is.

I've got a guy like that in one of my emerging markets. I was confronted by the other party, which threatened to sue me for something ridiculous. I calmly told them to call my attorney. All I had to do was mention his name, and the whole matter was dropped! How cool is that: *I didn't even have to pay the junkyard dog for that service!*

PROPERTY INSPECTOR

I think you're getting the hang of the underlying theme here: Find a property inspector with *demonstrated experience* in the type of property you're buying.

However, here's a new twist: Do *not* get your local property inspector as a referral from the broker who brought you the deal. Though it doesn't happen often, there's a chance the inspector may overlook something to help make the deal happen. He just might be concerned that if it looks like he killed the deal, he won't get any more business from that broker.

Get a referral from your property manager or other members of your team instead. Make sure it's a local person, because each area has its own particular problems and building codes.

Do not go with the low-ball bid, unless that person has lots of experience and comes highly recommended. Let the inspector take all the time he needs to give you a thorough report.

Good inspectors are like detectives: They may see only a minor problem, but their experience tells them it's a symptom of a much bigger problem that might not even have happened yet. That combination of knowledge and skill only comes from years of experience and it's worth every single penny.

APPRAISERS

"Hey Dave, doesn't the bank take care of the property appraisal?"

Well, yes, they do. In fact, they usually will not allow your appraiser to conduct the bank appraisal. That's not why you want an appraiser on your team.

You want a solid second opinion. These people are on the front lines of what's going on in that market. They know the direction of the *Path of Progress*, and current prices for properties in just about every condition and location. The good ones also have years of trend information between their ears. Sometimes appraisers are also brokers, and that can work well. Ask around to find an experienced appraiser.

As far as the bank appraiser is concerned, find out from the bank when that person will be at your property. Meet the appraiser there. Offer to get whatever additional information the appraiser needs to complete the appraisal. Make it easy to do business with you, and the deal has a better chance of coming together. You might even form a relationship over time with that appraiser, whom you could use on future deals with other lenders.

LENDER

When you determine what type of deal you're doing, you will get a lender involved and start the process of getting financing for the deal.

We covered financing in depth in Chapter 8. These companies and individuals are obviously vital to your growth.

CONTRACTORS

I have a reasonable definition of *good* for contractors: They get the job done on time and on budget. They respond to emergencies and charge you fairly. But no, I don't have a crystal ball for finding this rare breed.

I can tell you, however, that it's a mistake to *fall in love* with your contractor.

You will naturally gravitate to the company that does good work for you quickly and at a fair price. You'll definitely want to use that outfit over and over again. That's fine. What's not fine is when you stop taking bids from other contractors to get work done.

Your goal is not to get one good contractor, but to get three! They keep each other honest.

After starting from nothing, I began my real estate career doing rehabs for local banks. I was soon buying my own properties and rehabbing them for my own portfolio. Still, I continued to do work for banks and eventually got designated as a *Fannie Mae* and *Freddie Mac* contractor. This meant I could bid on Fannie Mae and Freddie Mac contractor work. And did they have work! They needed help with all the foreclosures they collected in the mid-to-late 1990s.

Even though I was a known and trusted team member, Fannie and Freddie would have me bid against two other quality contractors on *every job we did.* The other guys were just as good as I was: They did work on time, below budget, and they hustled just as hard. We all knew if we didn't do the job right, one of the other guys would get the next job.

There's another reason to get other bids every single time: When you continue to use the same contractor, you'll see the prices gradually rise. Each time it will be subtle until, before you know it, they're at the height of the market.

You don't mind the first bump or two in price, because you have such a great relationship. Then one day you wake up and realize you're simply being overcharged for work.

Be upset with *yourself.* It's you who didn't keep the contractor honest.

Remember my earlier advice on contractors: The fastest way to lose good ones is to make them chase you for money. They know they're good, they have plenty of business, and won't bid another job for you. Want to score points? *Pay early.*

INSURANCE AGENT

Good insurance agents will not only make sure you're covered, but will also find ways to get you maximum coverage at minimum cost. They'll keep you updated on changes that affect your business, including both opportunities and things to watch out for.

The good ones realize that saving you money on premiums may lower their current compensation, but you'll be a happy customer for years to come. You might even refer business to them.

$100,000 Lost over a Bottle of Wine

I went to my agent's office one December to plan our strategy for the coming year. While in his office I saw a couple of open wine cases.

A few days later, I saw his secretary in the local supermarket. On a hunch, I said: "Bob sure is giving away an awful lot of wine—does he do that for all his clients?" She said "Oh no, he only gives wine to his *special* clients." She didn't realize that I hadn't been given a bottle of wine.

At the time I owned a business, several vehicles, and nine multifamily properties. I was a contractor and landscaper, and got my hands dirty every day. I didn't rate a bottle from Bob.

I decided to move my business. One name popped up again and again: Lynch and Conboy in Brockton, Massachusetts. Dave Lynch and Marty Conboy treat *all* their clients like special clients, and I'm not talking just little things like gifts.

When I made the move, we sat down for a strategy session. They immediately saved me $14,000 on my premiums. They could have kept quiet and made all that cash. But they saw long-term value in the relationship.

Also look for agents that can really get things done. Early on, before I had all my systems in place, I would sometimes forget to take out an insurance binder. I'd be at the closing when the closing attorney would ask for it.

I would excuse myself and call Dave Lynch. Within minutes, the binder would be faxed over to the closing.

Over the years, they've made well over $100,000 servicing my accounts. And it might never have happened were it not for that 20-buck bottle of wine I didn't get.

DEMOGRAPHER

A good demographer will help you pinpoint emerging markets. She'll let you know when trends are going in your favor (time to get in), or in the opposite direction (time to get out).

In my book, *Emerging Real Estate Markets*, I take you step by step through the four phases of an emerging market. You discover when markets are in transition, and what strategies to use in each stage so you can maximize your profits at all times.

Demographers do the same thing, though they'll cost you a heck of a lot more! The great thing about experienced demographers is that they can tell you exactly what tenant profile is within a three-mile radius of your repositioning property.

That knowledge is critical to the success of your repositioned property. If you upgrade the property to the wrong tenant profile, you'll be trying to attract people from that three-mile radius, when in reality you will be repelling.

If you plan on doing any type of construction, definitely hire an experienced demographer. You can then pinpoint exactly what type of multi-family housing the market needs most.

Don't fall into the trap of renovating a property to the standard that *you* want to live in. You may or may not reflect that local market. Renovate the property to the local market.

I paid a visit to a property I had recently bought. It was a 72-unit C property in a B neighborhood.

It needed a little repositioning. I had 17 vacant units that needed repairs. After I had the new manager do a repair list for each unit, I was surprised to discover the extent of the repairs she recommended. This warranted a visit.

As we walked the units, I realized she wanted to replace appliances that didn't really need replacing. It was the same story with carpet that only needed steam cleaning, and vinyl flooring that would be fine with just a good scrubbing.

Then it all made sense: She said she wanted to renovate each unit as if she would live there. That was not what I wanted to hear about a C property!

I explained that this was a C property and she would not be a C tenant. Anyone can upgrade to the best. It takes skill to upgrade economically to the level that tenants are willing and able to pay for. At first I thought she might quit or think I would fire her, but to my surprise, she came around. We agreed on B-level improvements. I'm happy to report that she's doing a great job!

A strong demographer will help you avoid missing the correct magnitude of improvements.

1031 SPECIALISTS

As they say, *It's not how much you make, but how much you keep.*

Uncle Sam has quietly given us real estate investors a big present. He allows us to take all our profit from selling a property and plow it all back into another property as a down payment. And don't worry about taxes—just pay those when you decide to pull your money out of real estate.

There may be plenty of things messed up with big government, but this is not one of them! This process is called a *Section 1031 Tax-Deferred Exchange*, and it's not a loophole. It's written into the law.

And can it ever explode your wealth! You can buy a property with little or none of your own money, and then turn *all of the proceeds*—tax deferred—into a down payment on another property. This has the potential to multiply your equity by 5, 10, or even 20 times over the course of three or four exchanges.

Naturally, there are rules you must follow. Here's a summary of the key ones:

- *They must be like-kind exchanges.* It's not okay to go from an apartment to a boat. But it's fine to go from single-family property (not your home) to multi-family, or multi-family to commercial.
- *You must identify your replacement property within 45 days.* The clock starts ticking when you close on the sale of your existing property.
- *You must close on your new property within 180 days.* This clock also starts when you close on the sale of that existing property, and it's not negotiable with the IRS. They're so strict that even if the 180th day falls on a holiday, you'd better close the day before, not one day after.
- *You must use an intermediary.* These firms specialize in 1031 exchanges. Your intermediary will handle all the paperwork and movement of funds. You—or even your attorney—can *never* touch the funds during the exchange. They cannot enter a bank account controlled primarily by you. Otherwise, the exchange is voided.

Do background checks on your intermediary. There are many good ones, but also some crooks (surprise!). The industry is not licensed, but should be. If you want a list of some of the larger specialists, just go to MultiFamilyMillions.com and type in the keyword 1031.

Your specialist will give you complete guidelines to follow, tailored to your situation. Yes, the rules can be complicated. That's the job of the specialist to keep you on top of them.

Believe me, it's worth it! The combination of investing in multifamily properties in emerging markets, repositioning them for maximum value, and using your right to a 1031 exchange—well, it's the best recipe I know to explode your wealth.

ACCOUNTANT

Behind every wealthy real estate investor is an unsung hero known as the accountant. Certified Public Accountants perform many functions for you. They:

- File required reports to the government.
- Prepare and send in your quarterly and year-end tax returns.
- Advise you on the tax consequences of any transactions or changes you're planning.

In short, the good ones will advise you on the best way to increase your wealth while staying within the bounds of the IRS.

You won't end up with the same accountant you started out with. That's because you'll outgrow them.

At first you might do your own taxes, or have someone like H & R Block™ do them for you. As you acquire several properties, your taxes become more complicated.

Now it's time to move up. You might get referred to a specialist who works out of her house. She has a good reputation and many investors use her.

Then your appetite gets even larger, and you branch out into other businesses. For instance, maybe you become a real estate broker yourself, or have a rehabbing operation in addition to your investments.

You'll then need someone who's dealt with such rapidly expanding operations before. If you stick with the existing person—who was just right when you were smaller—you risk not taking advantage of tax strategies available at this level of business. Even worse, you might miss some paperwork that's necessary.

If you get fairly big, you'll use the tax services of a large company. They'll have many specialists under one roof, and will create a tax team within the company to work on your account.

How do you know when you've outgrown your current accountant? Keep that person for now, but each year have your taxes reviewed by a bigger company. Ask that company whether it could have saved you more money. This approach will cost you extra money for the additional review. But at some point, the savings from stepping up to the next level will more than cover your cost.

You may even end up with more specialists on your team than I've outlined in this chapter. They might include a public adjuster, marketing expert, web specialist, and others. But for now, just focus on getting these key people in place. They're the secret to avoiding problems, maximizing your opportunities, and making you wealthier than all of them put together!

IN THE NEXT CHAPTER

If I've done my job, right now you're experiencing two emotions: You're excited about jumping in and finding your first repositioning deal, and even though we're near the end of the book, you still might have a few questions.

Fortunately, there are a number of resources you can tap to get those questions answered. It's going to be great when you're part of the small-but-very-rich community of investors who reposition apartments. Find out more about these resources in the next chapter.

CHAPTER 15

NEXT STEPS ON YOUR ROAD TO WEALTH

I discovered a long time ago that successful people do two things unsuccessful people don't do:

1. They continue to educate themselves.
2. They take action.

You've just proven that you are willing to educate yourself, or you wouldn't have bothered to buy and read this book. Now it's time to take the next step and put what you've discovered into action.

People ask me all the time what they must do to get started. You have enough to get started right now!

You must apply the steps I gave you and get your phone to ring. You do that by beginning your marketing. Create some relationships. Open your eyes to the properties you might have driven by a thousand times. And start to analyze deals. Just as sailors need to get their *sea legs* so they're comfortable at sea, you need your real estate legs. By analyzing deal after deal—even if they're just on loopnet.com and you don't intend to buy them—you'll begin to understand your market.

Your first steps will be tentative. You will definitely reach many dead ends. People will tell you "no," or not even bother to get back to you.

So what! By taking these simple actions—and by continuing in the face of slow going, rejection, and uncertainty—you are paying the price of success. Each rejection or dead end is a place where your competition turns around and goes home, but you continue on.

I've covered in this book a lot of systems that will help you grow your fortune quickly. No doubt you'll create other systems that work just right for you. Please don't fall into the trap of creating them first.

Too many people think *my situation's different,* and they don't follow proven systems. Then, when their cobbled-together attempt fails, they say: "See . . . I *told* you it wouldn't work!" Be smarter than that: First follow the recipe to bake that cake. Don't second-guess it; just follow it exactly! Then when you've baked a few of them, you have the credentials to experiment. Not before.

Michael Gerber has a great book called *The E-Myth Revisited.* It could help you with creating systems in your business, so you don't make the same mistake twice.

I suspect that you'd be disappointed if everything I ever learned about real estate investing were in this one book. That's not the case, of course.

I've been asked just about every imaginable question about real estate investing. To tell you the truth, I got tired answering them after a while! Many are good questions, but you know Old Dave by now—I started looking for a way to systematize my answers. So I created some kits you can take home and use to continue your study of real estate investing.

For instance, one course is called *Apartment House Riches.* It comes with a 172-page manual, all kinds of ready-made checklists, and audio CDs so you can turn the waiting time in your car into profitable time. And when you implement those concepts, pretty soon you'll be able to quit that commute!

I even include my proprietary *Multi-Unit Profit Finder*™ software, so you run those real estate calculations at lightning speed. Let the computer do the boring calculations. The software even gives you a *red light* or a *green light* on key calculations, making it easy to tell if you're looking at a good deal.

Because you got off your duff and made it this far in my book, I've got a special offer that you can get only at: MultiFamilyMillions.com when you type in the keywords *special offer.*

HOW IMPATIENT ARE YOU?

Believe me when I say that you don't need my home study kit to become successful. This book gave you the guidance you need to assemble your team and start your investing career.

It's just that some people are more impatient than others. They're the ones who walk right by the delicious Duncan Hines™ complete cake mix box, and go right to the bakery to pick up a cake. Hey, the box and a couple of eggs are all you need to make the cake. But they just want the cake.

So if you're moderately impatient, I recommend the home study course. It gives you even more shortcuts—including that special software—to save you time on your profit journey.

What if you're *really* impatient? What if you're sick to death of your day job, and that's why you're staying up late, reading this book? You could consider attending a live training event.

I hold these events several times each year in different cities. You get me live for three or four days. Sometimes, people are so filled with questions that they really benefit from the live training: I not only answer every single question they have, but they get to hear my answers to everyone else's questions!

We also do a ton of case studies. We start with the smaller deals, and you calculate whether it's a good one or not. I then describe my take on that deal and why I like it or not. Then we do the same for larger deals, all the way up to a $7 million one. Pretty soon you're running those calculations like an *old hand*. In fact, when you walk out of the event and return home, you have zero concerns about analyzing deals, because you have already analyzed so many!

My boot camp students tell me that the reason they are so wildly successful when leaving the boot camps is because when they do their first deal, it's more like they're doing their sixth or seventh deal because of the amount of case studies that we do.

I have live events for investing in apartments and also for attracting all the private money you will ever need to do *your* deals with *other people's* money. Simply go to MultiFamilyMillions.com and type in the keywords *live event* for more information on these opportunities.

No one was teaching these powerful investing techniques when I started out. That's probably the reason I bought only three-unit to six-unit properties for the first four years of my career. If I knew then what I know now—that doing big deals is just as easy as doing small ones—I would have done bigger deals sooner! And life would have been easier, faster!

THE ABSOLUTE SHORTEST SHORTCUT TO REAL ESTATE WEALTH

Here's how you do it:

1. You read this book (hey, you get to cross that one right off!).
2. You now go out there and start applying the principles you discovered.
3. If you have the resources, you further your training through either home study courses or live events (they don't have to be mine; they just have to be with the very best experts you can find).
4. You get a mentor to hold you accountable.

Let's talk about this last one: People who achieve great success have another thing in common—they find one or more mentors who get them to their goals faster.

Mentors or coaches are not just for beginners. Michael Jordan always had a coach, and so does Tiger Woods. To this day, I have coaches and mentors on whom I constantly rely for advice—and sometimes a kick in the pants. These specialists have *been there and done that,* as the saying goes. The good ones are like shortcuts on legs.

They also don't shy away from holding you accountable. Imagine the momentum you build up when you have a coach who is just as committed to your success as you are. This person keeps you accountable every two weeks so you know what steps are necessary to reach your goal. No excuses, no procrastinating.

I do have a coaching program with students from across the United States. They're from all walks of life, and all economic backgrounds. They're in the fastest lane toward success because someone is continually there to guide them. Their coaches help them to develop their action plans and keep them accountable to make those action plans a reality. Again, mentors or coaches are not a requirement for success; they simply accelerate it.

To find out more about my coaching program, simply go to MultiFamilyMillions.com and type in the keyword *coaching*.

BONUS MATERIALS FOR YOU

As it says on the cover of this book, I have a package of bonuses I'd like to send you in the mail. They'll give you additional information on multi-family investing.

Why would I offer bonuses? It's simple: Most people don't take action to make their dreams a reality, and I respect the ones who do. So if you want your kit, just go to MultiFamilyMillions.com and type in the keywords *bonus pack*. I'll get it right out to you. (By the way, I will never sell, rent, or give your name to anyone else. This is not some scam to harvest your name. It's just a bonus from one real estate investor to another.)

Abe Lincoln once said: "Things may come to those who wait—but only the things left by those who hustle."

I enjoyed sharing my knowledge with you. Now it's up to you to get out there and use it! Not *if* but *when* you're successful, please contact me and share your success story!

INDEX